Quentin Blake

Tell Me A Picture

FRANCES LINCOLN

in association with National Gallery Company, London

For Stan and Cynthia

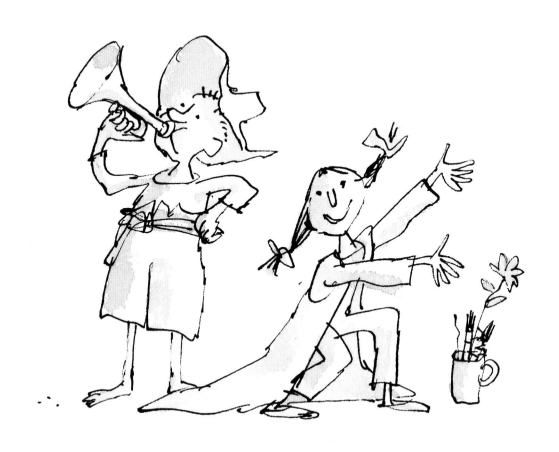

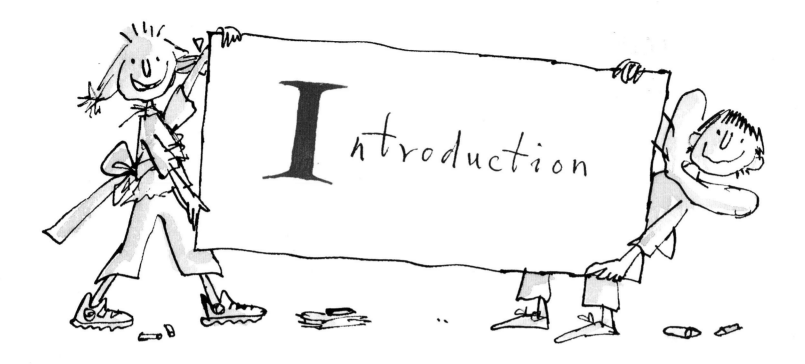

Introduction

This book has been published to accompany an exhibition of the same title, but it has a life of its own apart from the exhibition. In it you will find pictures from the National Gallery selected by Quentin Blake and surrounded by his drawings: in these drawings we meet a series of characters who respond to the pictures in the kind of way only children can – to the very essence of what is going on in them.

When Quentin Blake was appointed the first Children's Laureate, it was in recognition of his work as inspirational writer and illustrator of books for the young. The job also entails the delightful duty of raising the profile of writing and drawing for children 'in whatever way the Laureate considers appropriate'. Happily for the National Gallery, Blake quickly realised that his ideal 'appropriate way' would be to communicate to a young public his conviction that looking at great illustrations can be the first step on the journey towards enjoyment of great paintings. He conceived the idea of an exhibition that would include both these kinds of art; and this is where the *Tell Me A Picture* project began.

The National Gallery has long believed that young children and Old Masters go together. After all, the pictures belong to the young just as much as to the old. Children, often in contrast to the adults who accompany them, arrive in the Gallery refreshingly unencumbered with preconceptions about art. They do not feel obliged to like a painting simply because it was painted by a famous artist. Left to their own devices they will often be drawn to the curious, the unexpected or the mysterious and they will feel free to interpret and to imagine meaning and narrative: in other words they will engage at every level with the image that has attracted their attention.

The Children's Laureate's job description required the ability of the postholder to be able to enjoy the job. If evidence of this were needed, it is contained here in this book. I can guarantee that Quentin Blake's enjoyment will be shared by people of all ages who turn these pages.

Neil MacGregor
Director of the National Gallery

Author's acknowledgements

Tell Me A Picture would not have been possible without the support and enthusiasm of the Education Department of the London National Gallery. I owe thanks to all the staff of the Gallery and in particular to Ghislaine Kenyon, whose collaboration included not only providing most of the notes on individual paintings but also helpful discussion of every aspect of this book.

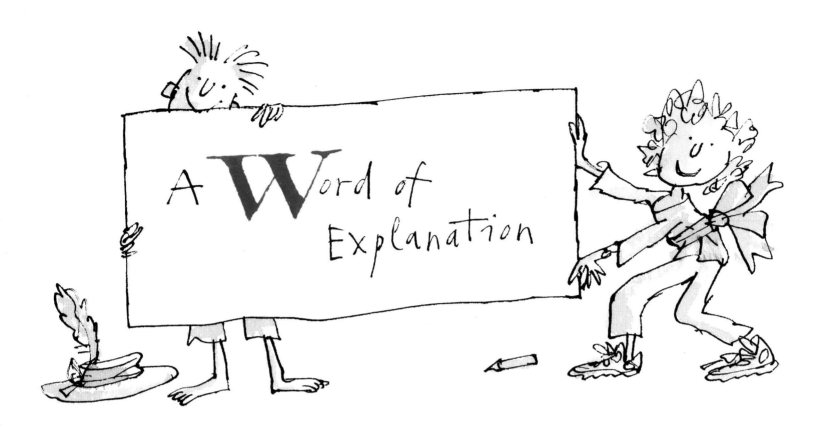

A Word of Explanation

Whether we think about it or not, looking at pictures is an important part of our lives. When we are young we look avidly at the pictures in storybooks, and beyond these is a wide panoply of other created images – so many that we almost come to take them for granted. However, it is not always easy to go from these pictures to the ones that people have felt worth preserving in museums and art galleries. We may eventually come to have a real affection for such places – I certainly do – but that doesn't mean that the first steps into them aren't sometimes a bit daunting.

That is one of the reasons why, when I became the first Children's Laureate in 1999 with a brief to do 'whatever I felt appropriate', I put forward the idea for an exhibition at the National Gallery in London and for this book, both called *Tell Me A Picture*.

Because I illustrate books, as well as sometimes writing them, I am always interested in stories; and so my first requirement for my choice of pictures here was that they should have some sense of story in them. Sometimes the exact nature of the story isn't clear, but then the invitation to imagine it may be all the stronger. In fact one of the main purposes of this book is just that: to invite you to think about what you feel is happening in these pictures.

It is not unusual to encounter books or exhibitions which are arranged by artist or artistic movement – Monet, the Surrealists – or by theme – landscape, still life, animals, war – and sometimes that arrangement is intended to lead our thoughts in a certain direction. Not so here. These pictures are arranged in alphabetical order; not for the sake of the alphabet, but so that they are in no order that has anything to do with one painting being more important than another, or more recent, or more respected. You are invited to look at them all just as pictures.

You will see that they are introduced by an assorted crew of conversational children, who first announce the name of the artist and afterwards generally can't resist a few observations and queries about the picture. Each of the pictures, however, has two pages to itself; and there you are on your own with the picture, so that your imagination can meet the imagination of the artist. It is quite possible that you will know some of the pictures already, and that others you will meet are quite new. As with people, you may instinctively like or dislike them before you know much about them. Later on – an hour later, a week later, a year later – you may want to know more about these artists and their works. There are dozens of places where you can enquire, and one place to start is with the notes at the back of this book. But leave them until you have looked at the pictures first!

When I chose the pictures for this book I was thinking of story as being what they have in common, but that doesn't mean that I wasn't also aware of their visual qualities. In fact the kinds of stories they suggest are inextricably mixed with these qualities. Each has its own flavour, its own kind of meaning. I think they are all good pictures.

Perhaps for this occasion twenty-six pictures are enough to think about; but beyond the pages of this book, there are so many more, of all times and places, waiting to be discovered by us and become an important part of our lives.

Quentin Blake

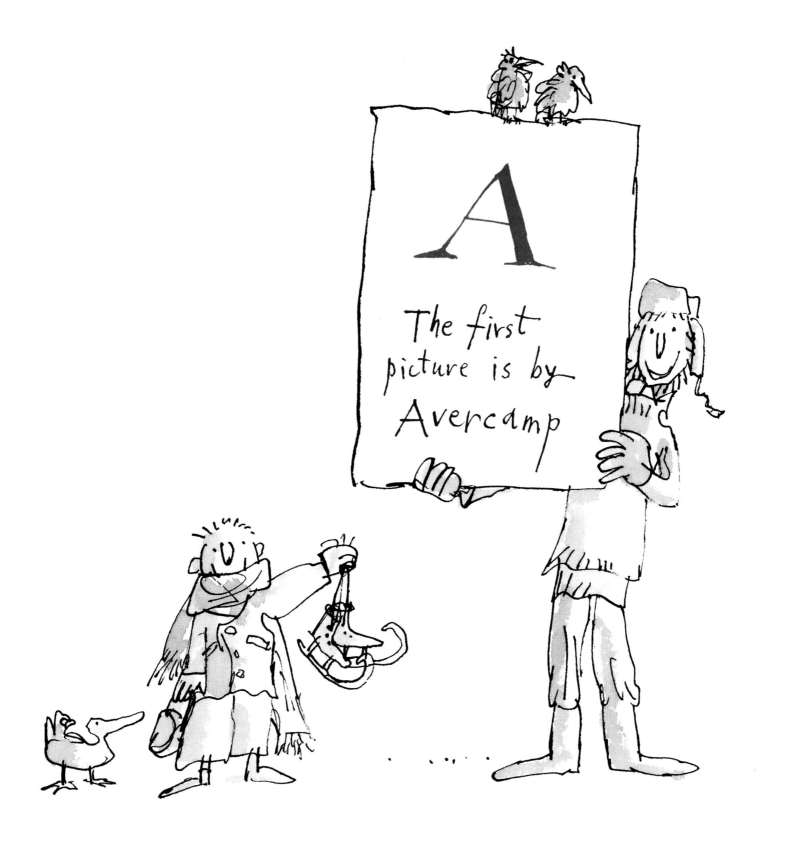

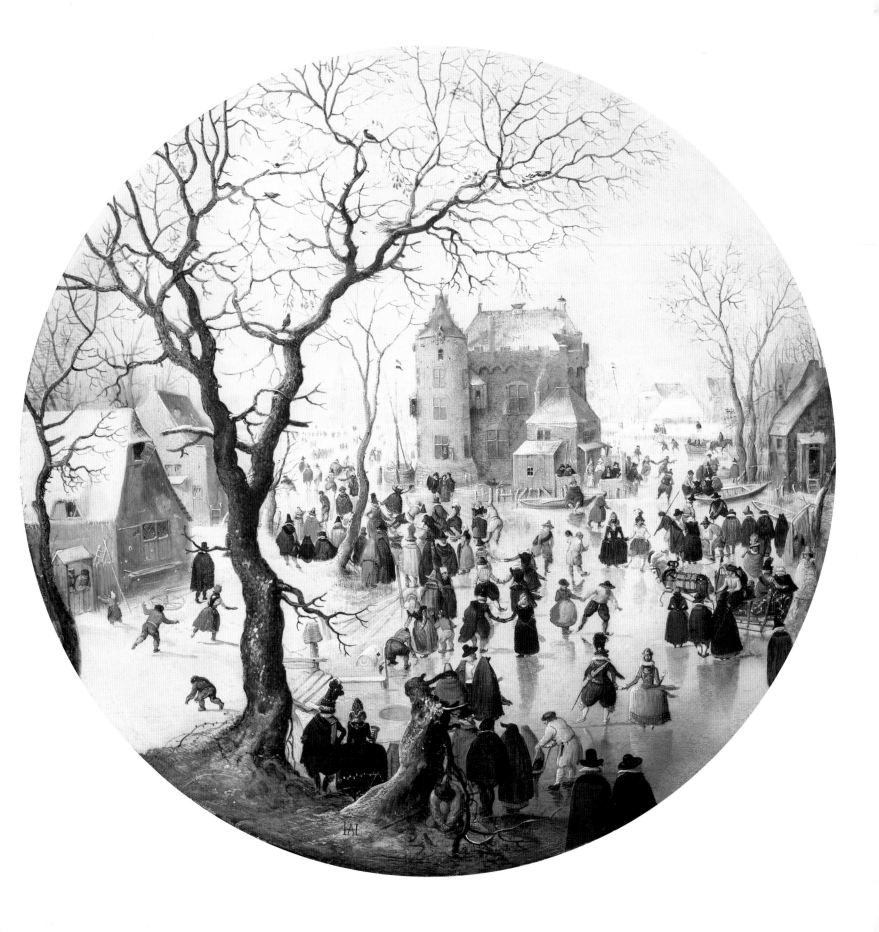

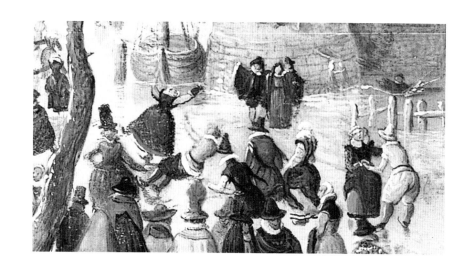

Did you notice that man who had fallen over?

I hope they don't fall through that hole in the ice.

It made us feel chilly.

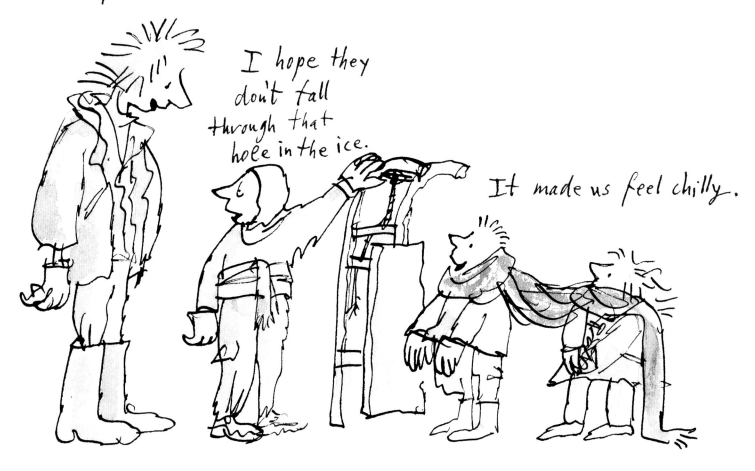

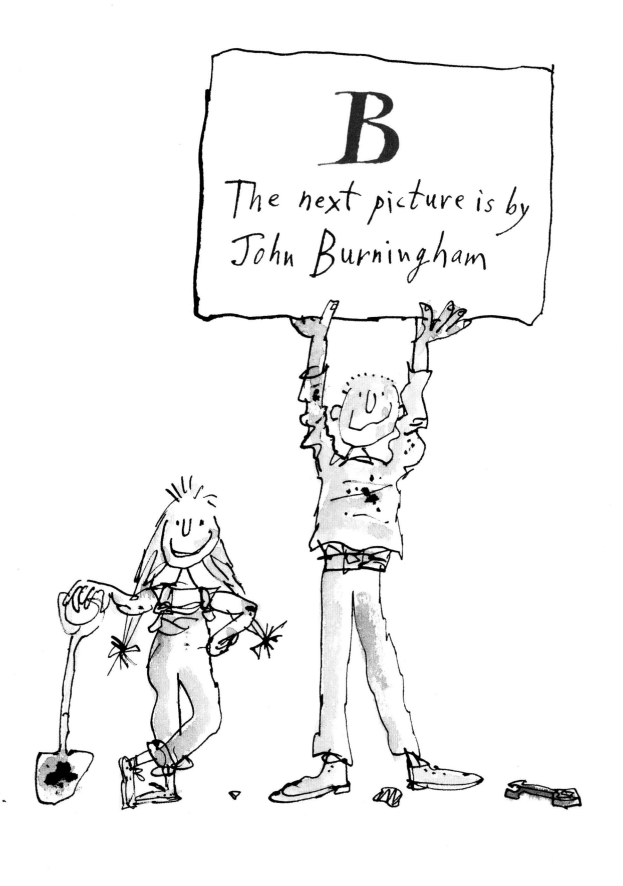

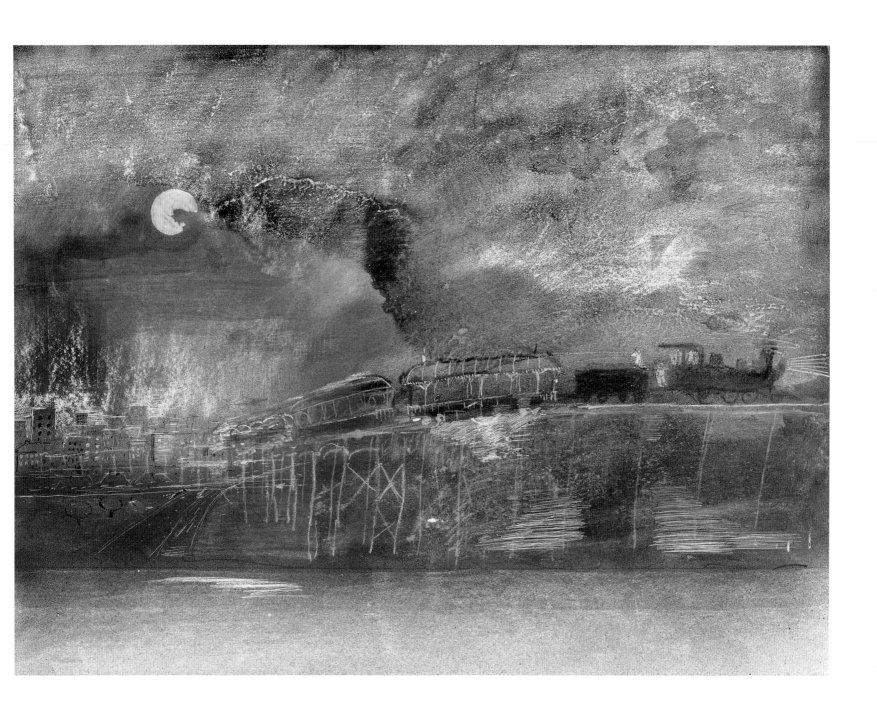

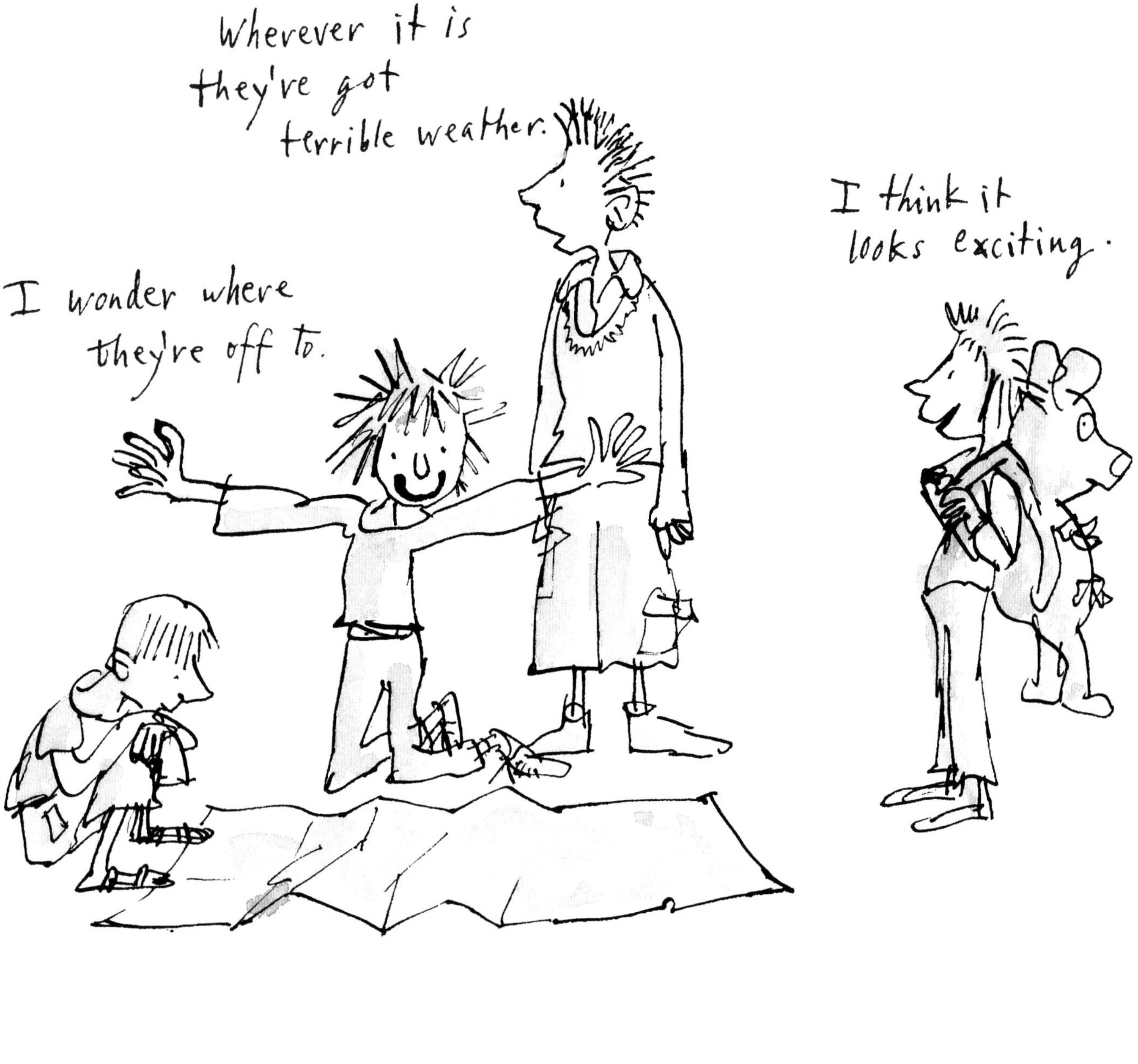
Wherever it is they're got terrible weather.
I wonder where they're off to.
I think it looks exciting.

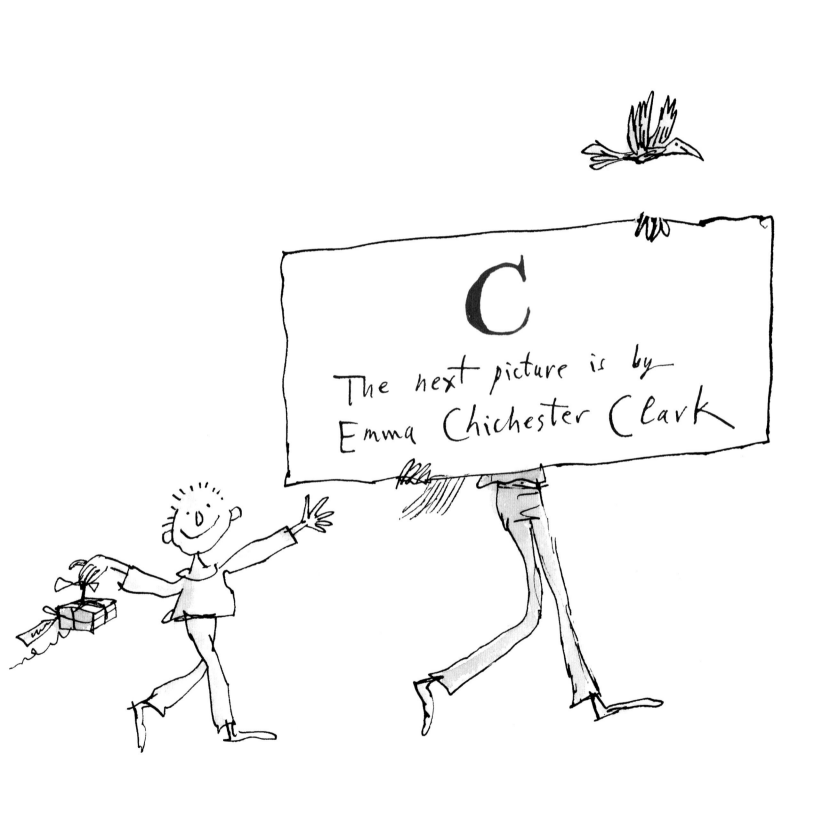

C

The next picture is by
Emma Chichester Clark

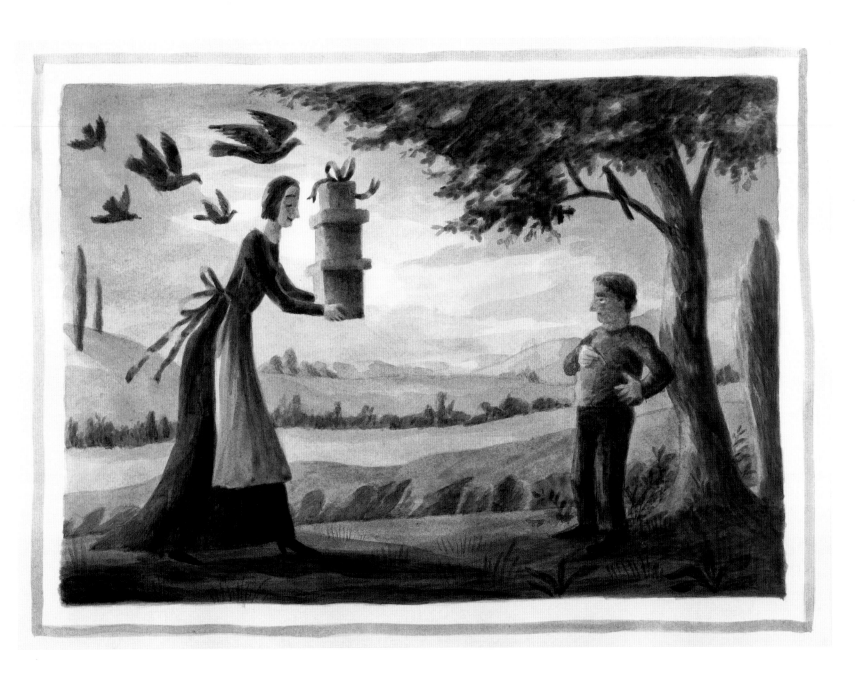

I wonder what's in
all those parcels.

Is it his
birthday?

I think
they're presents.

If they are he
doesn't look very
pleased to get them.

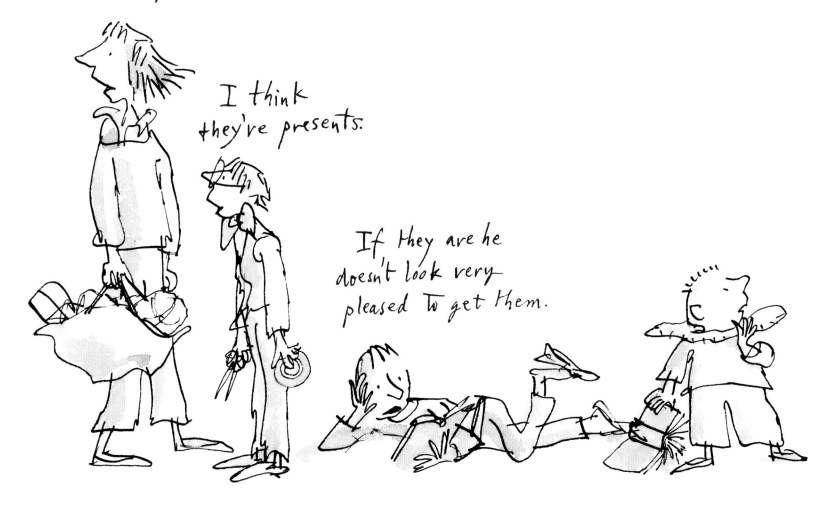

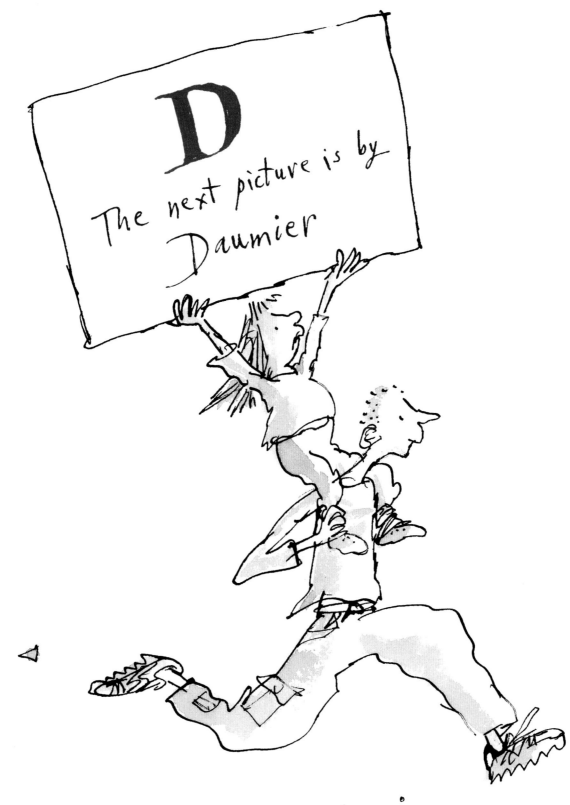

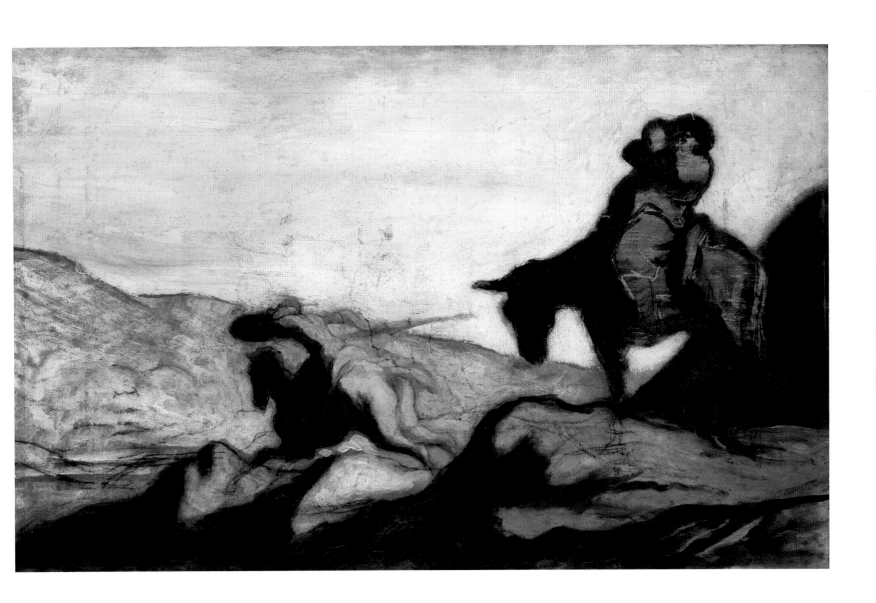

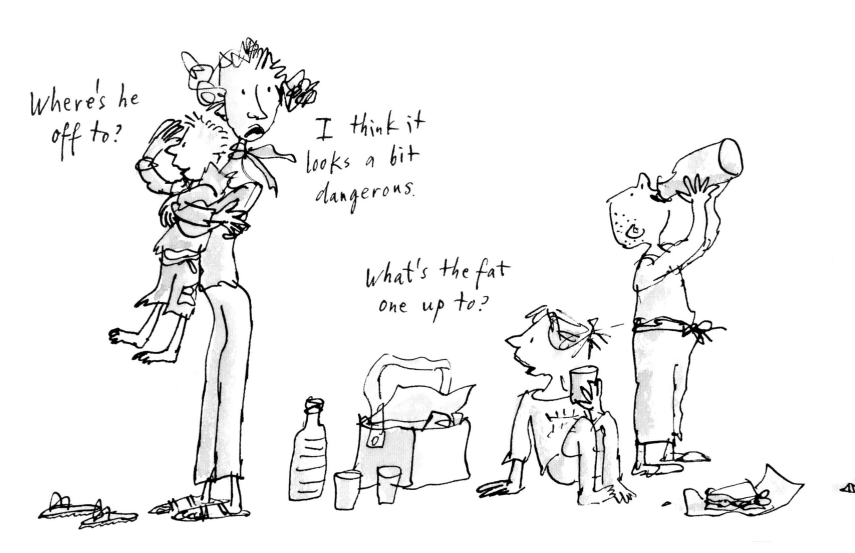

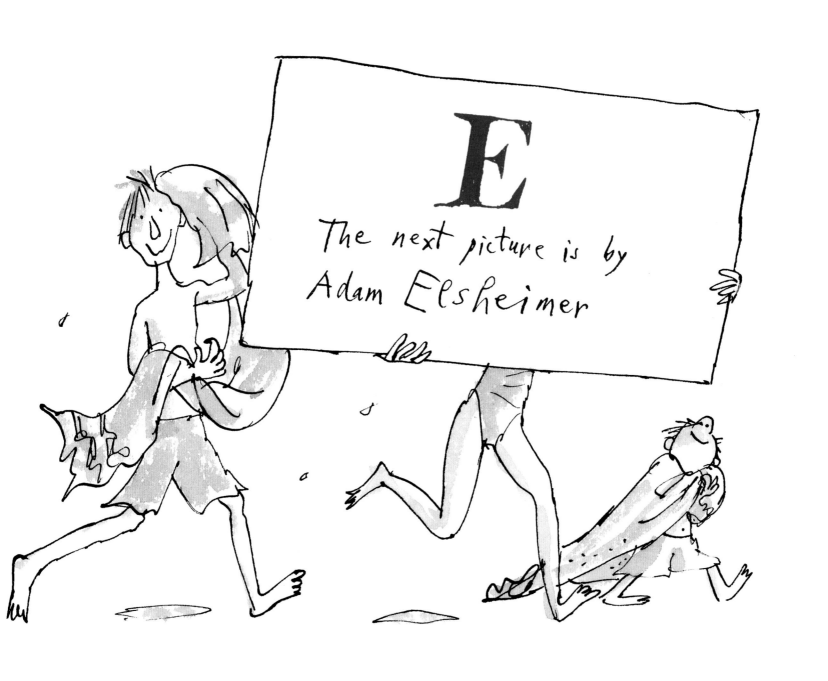

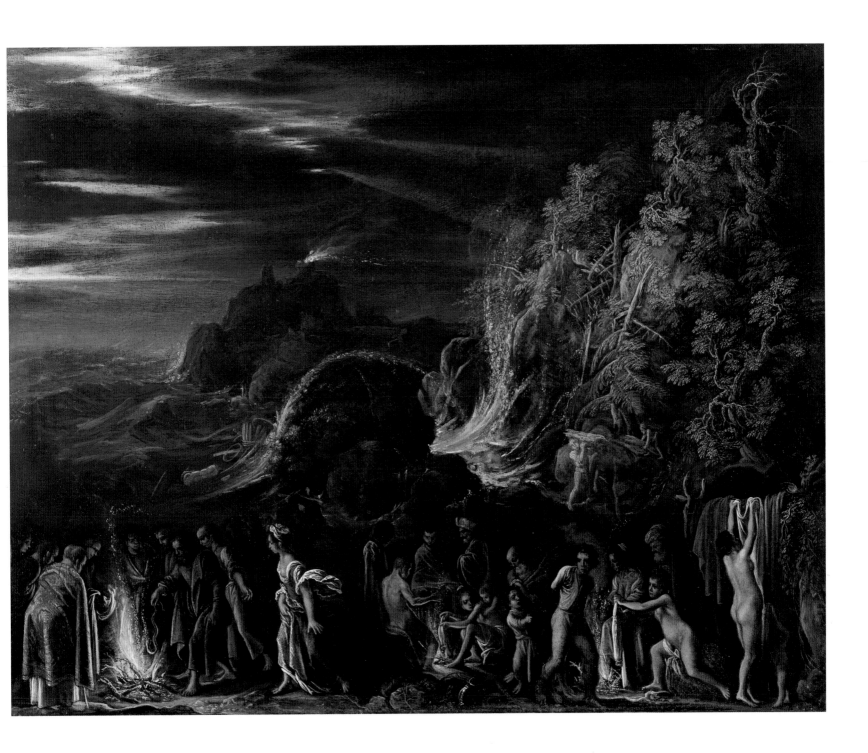

You have to look
very closely
to see what's
going on.

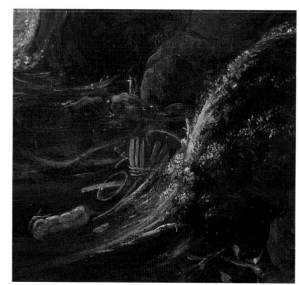

Some of them
look very
wet.

If they don't
take care they might
catch a chill.

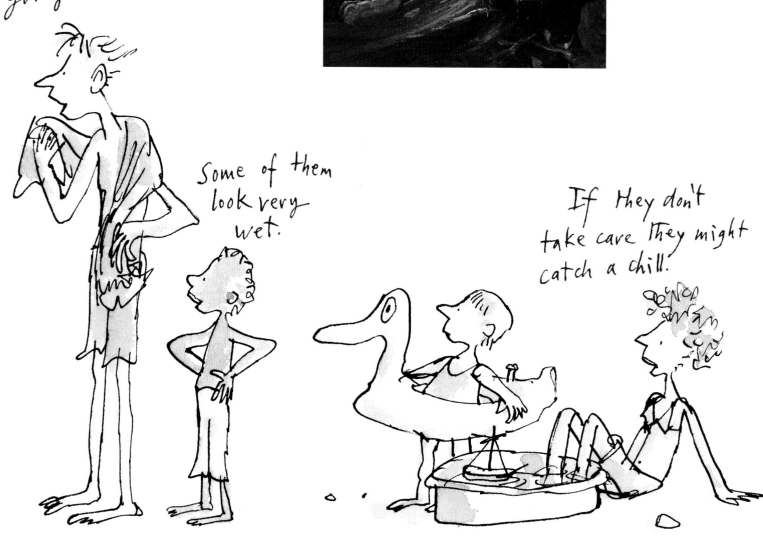

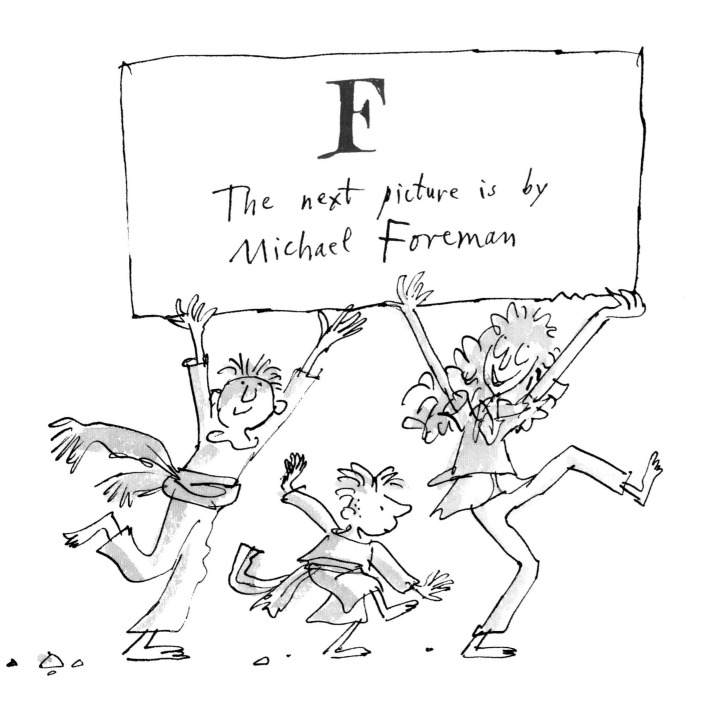

F

The next picture is by
Michael Foreman

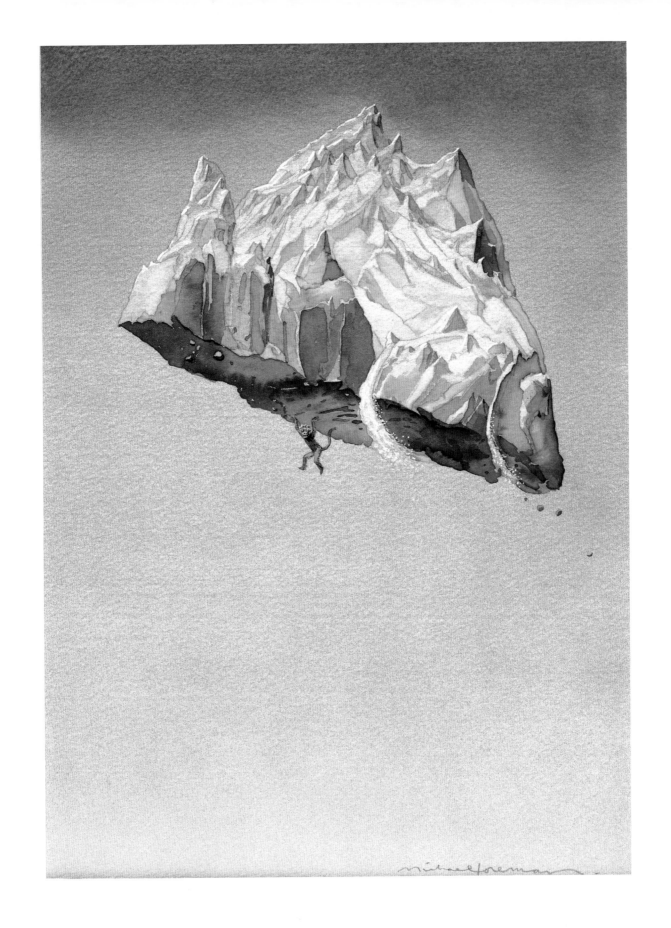

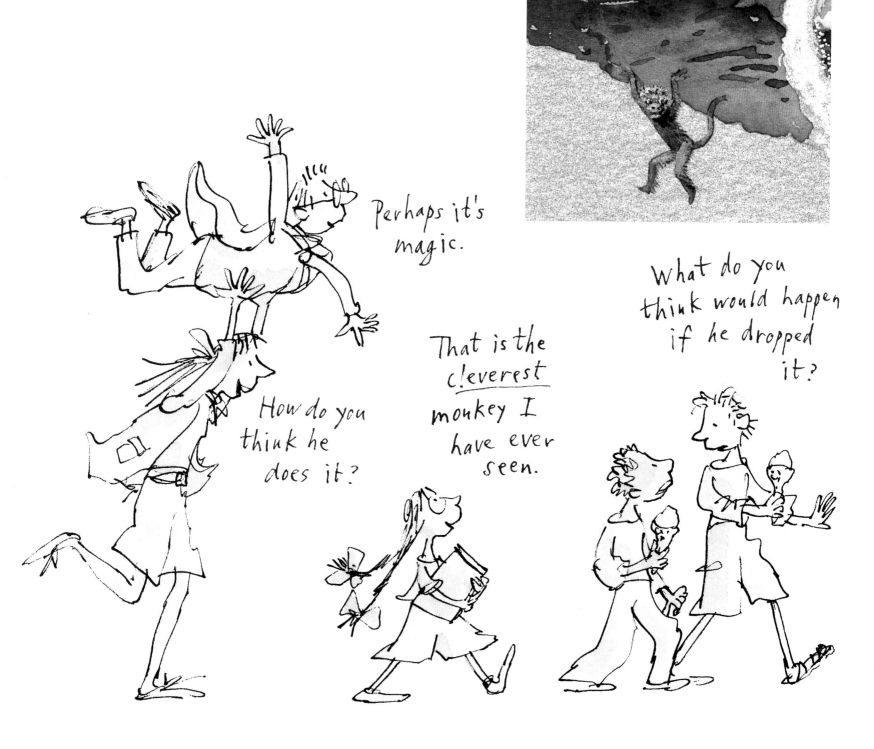

Perhaps it's magic.

What do you think would happen if he dropped it?

That is the _cleverest_ monkey I have ever seen.

How do you think he does it?

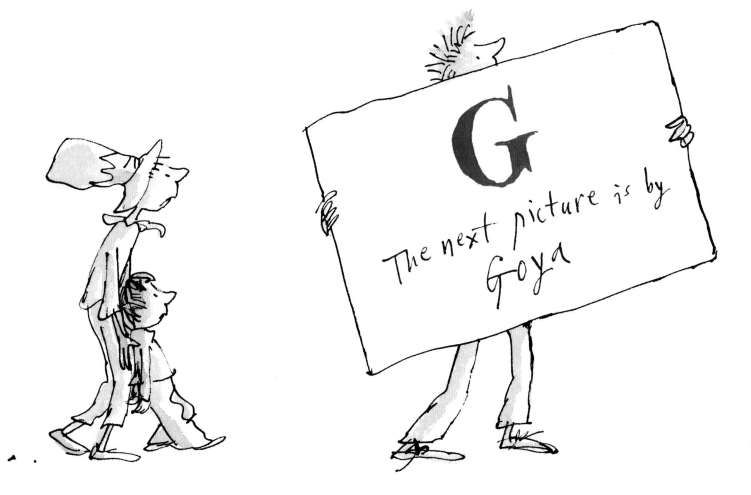

G

The next picture is by Goya

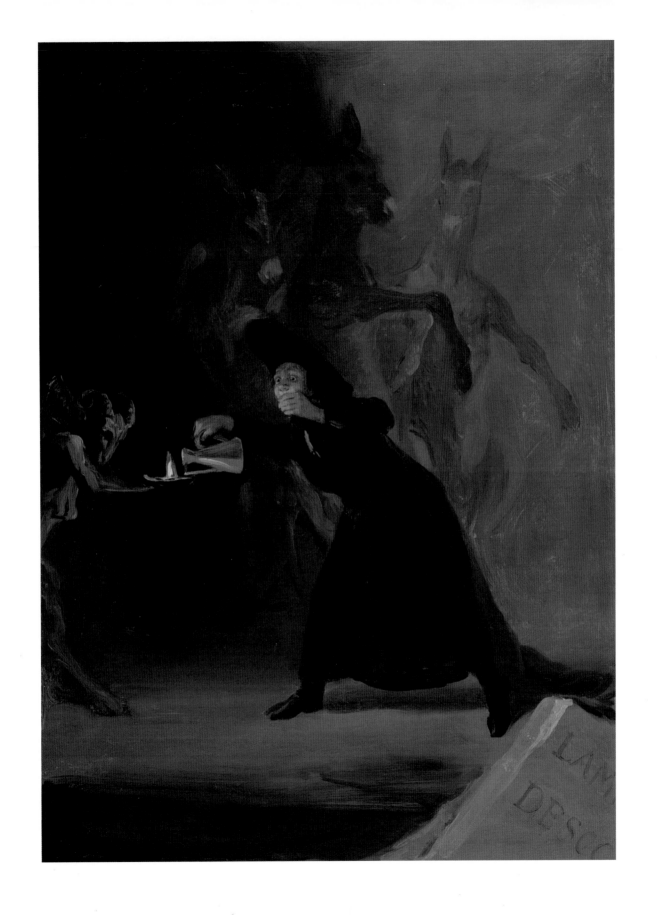

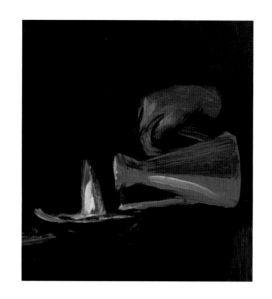

I don't know what's happening but it looks really bogey.

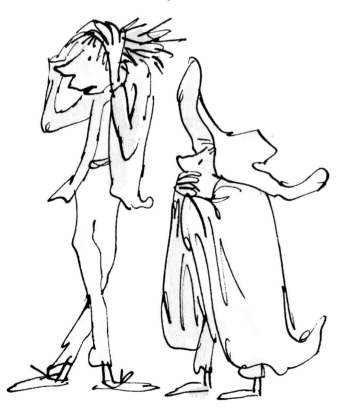

I had a dream like that once.

I hope I don't have one.

I liked it...

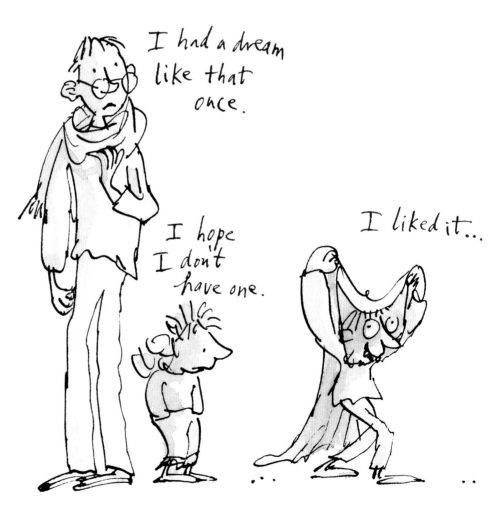

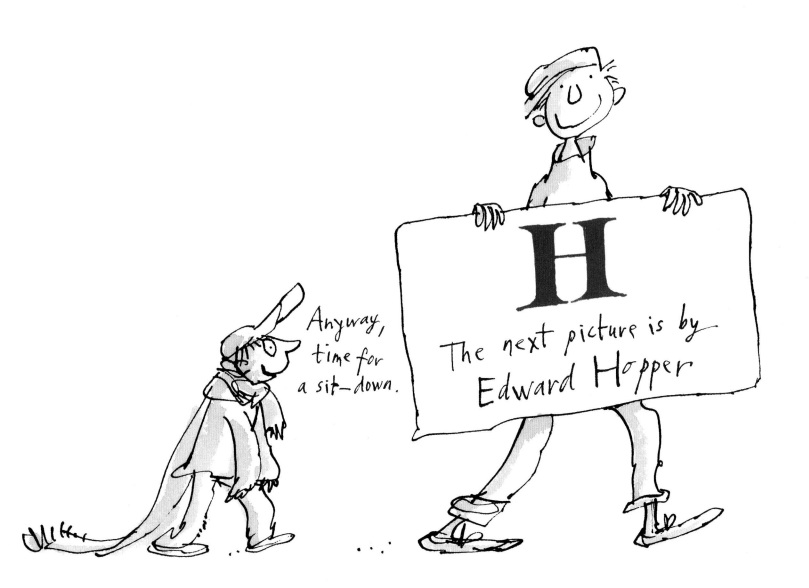

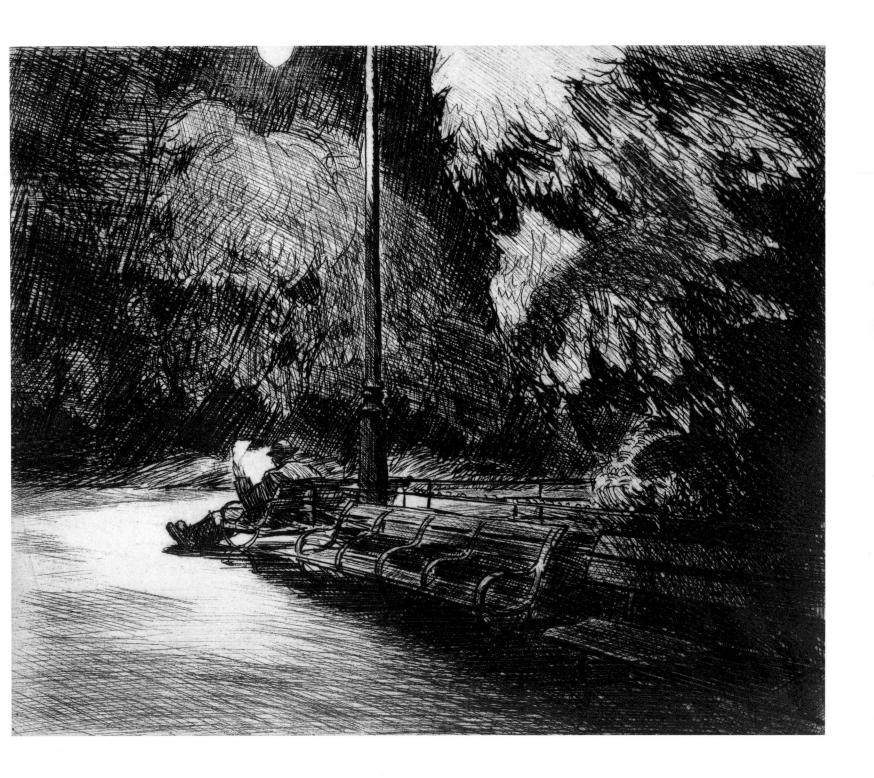

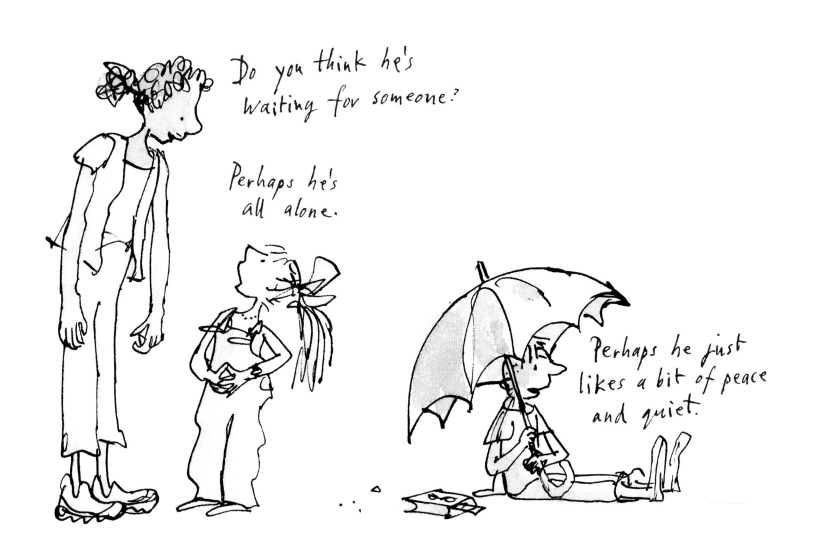

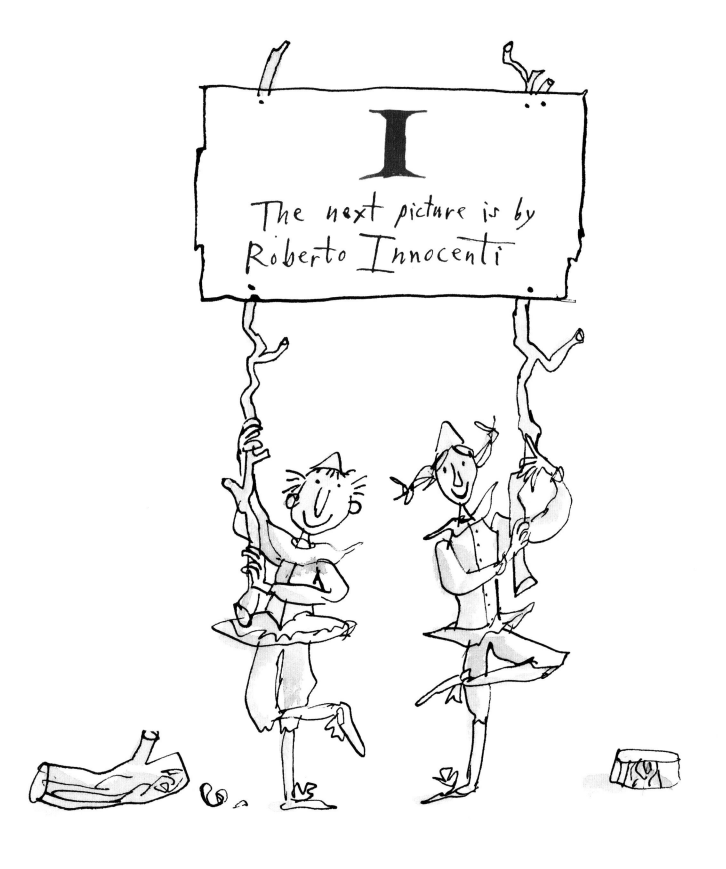

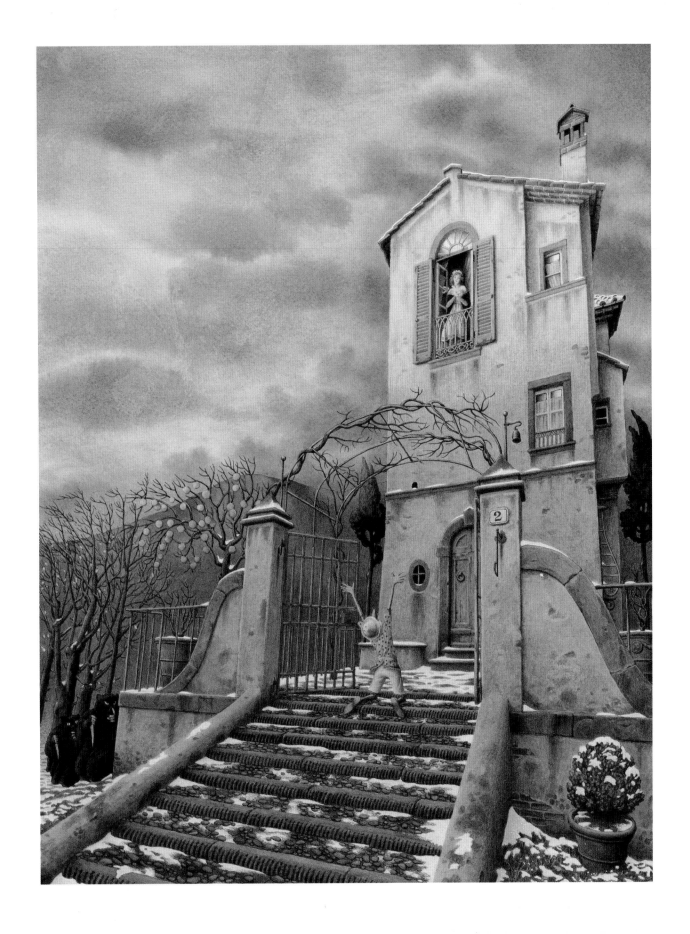

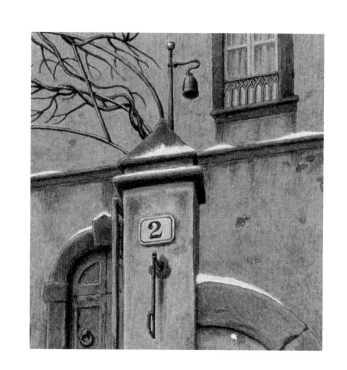

Do you think he knows about those two in the corner?

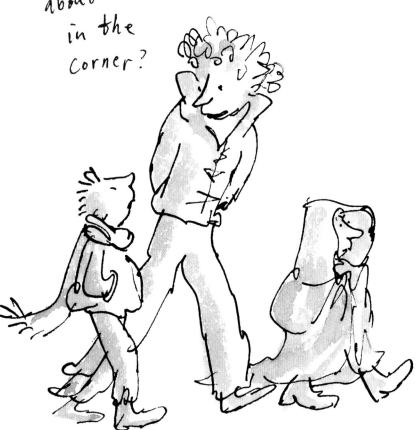

My friend used to live in a house exactly like that.

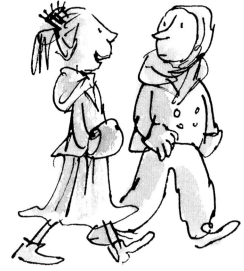

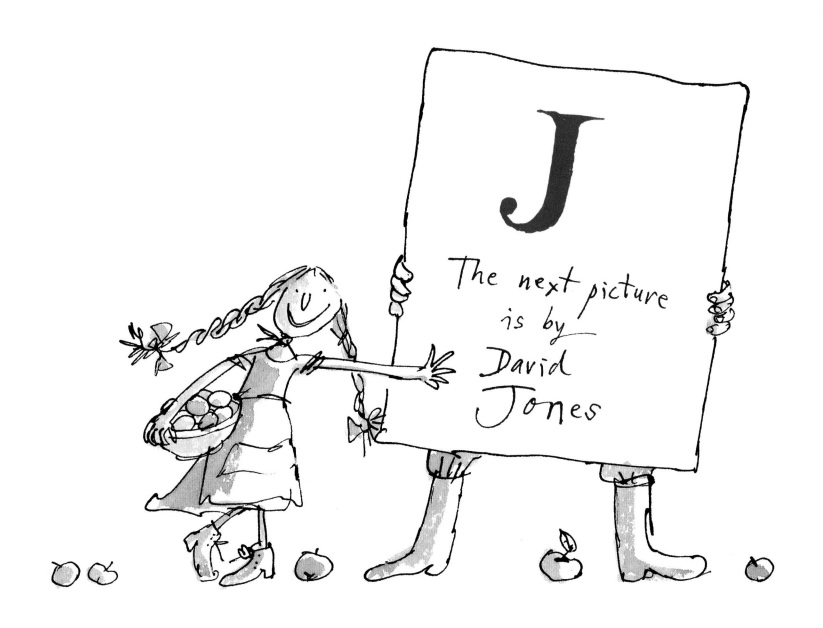

J

The next picture
is by
David
Jones

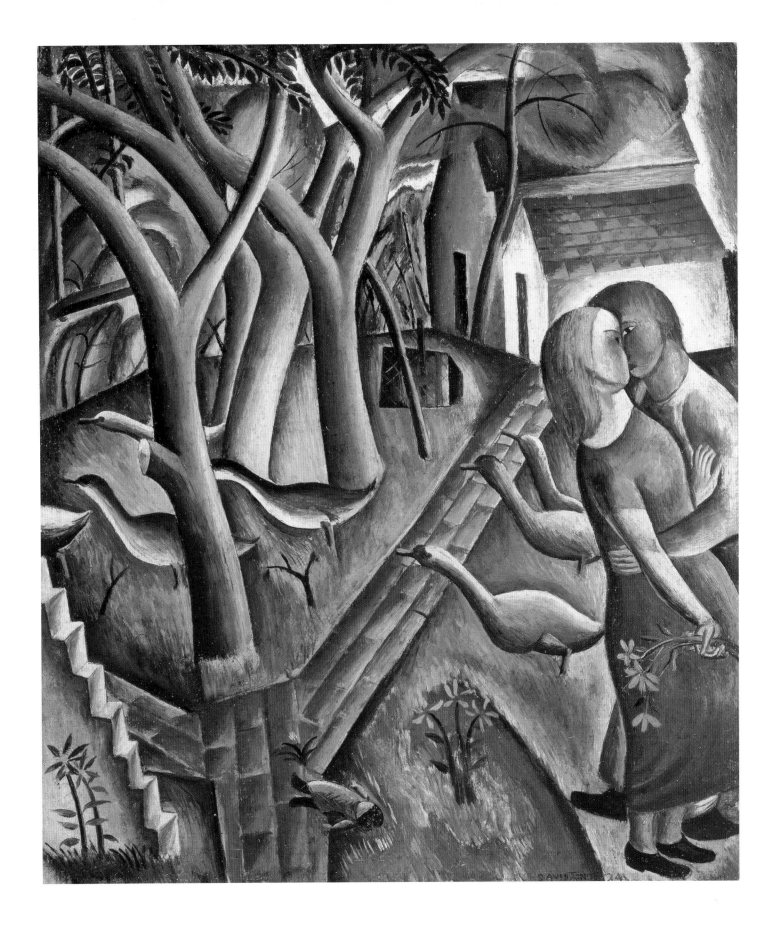

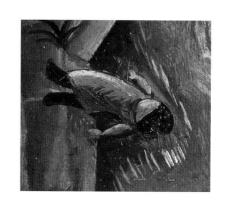

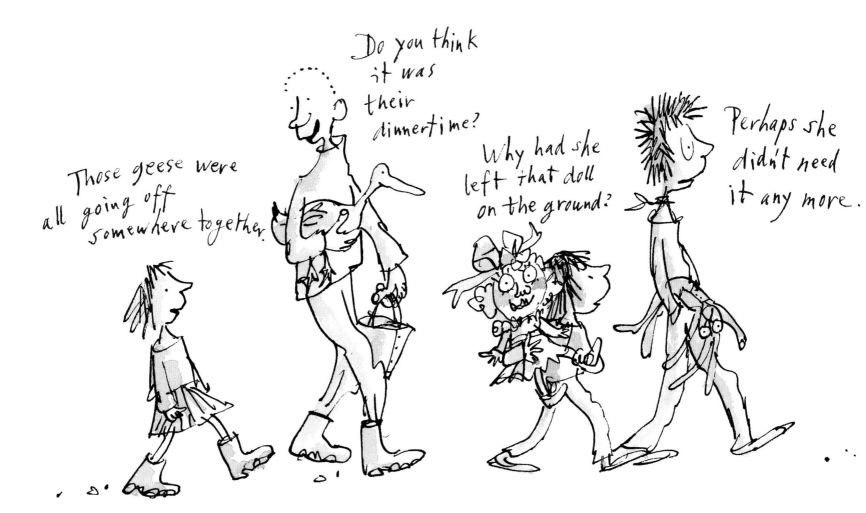

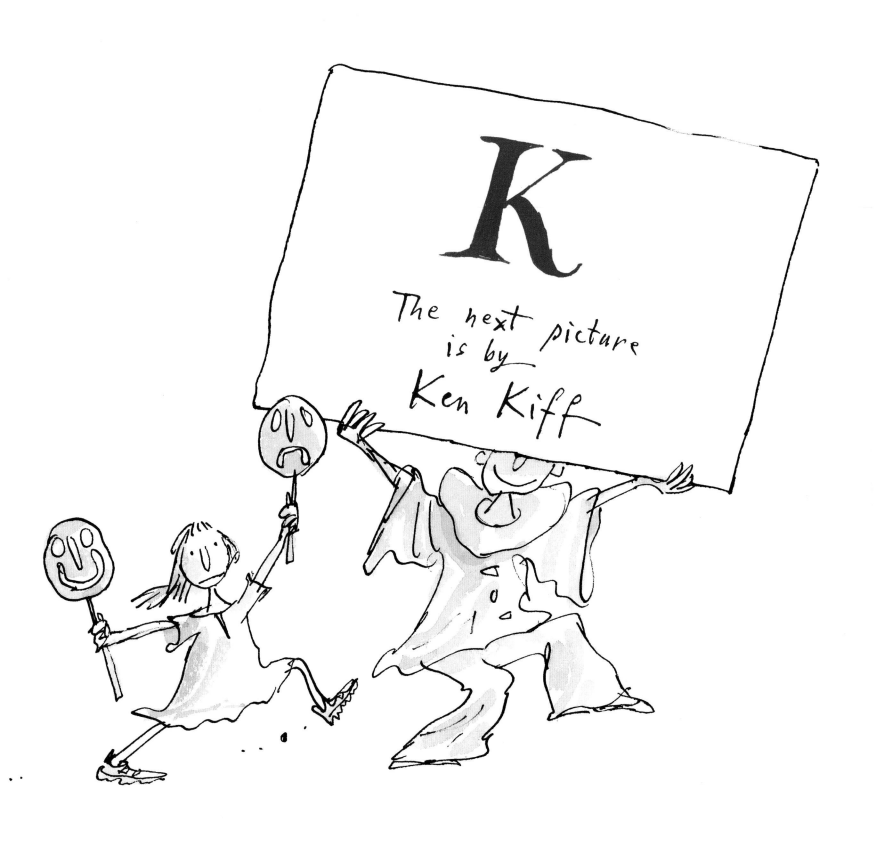

K

The next picture
is by
Ken Kiff

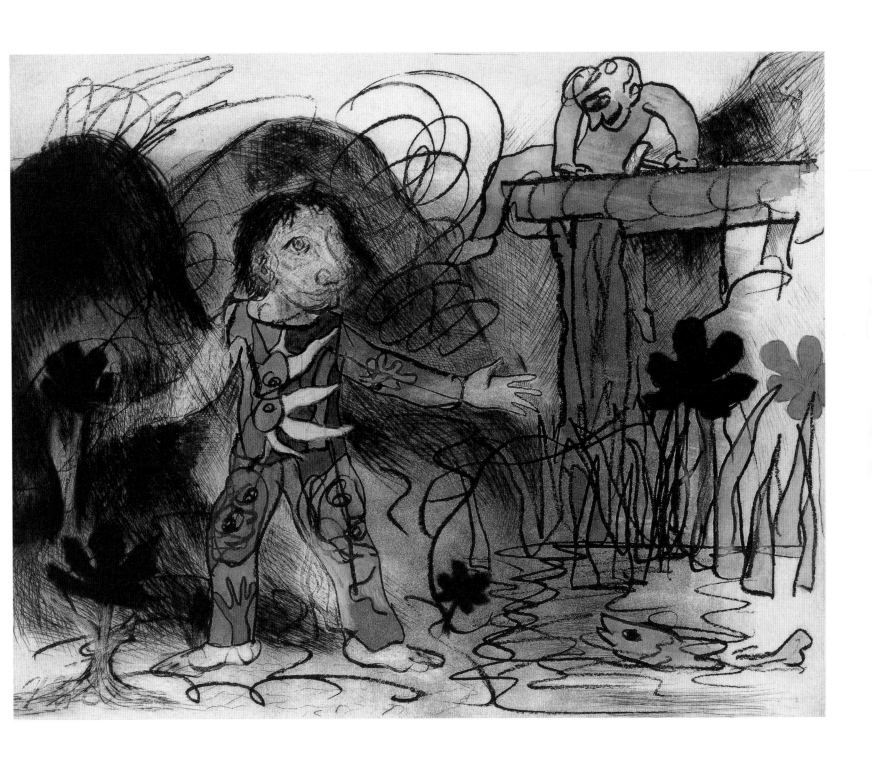

He doesn't look very happy. I wonder why not.

Clowns are like that sometimes.

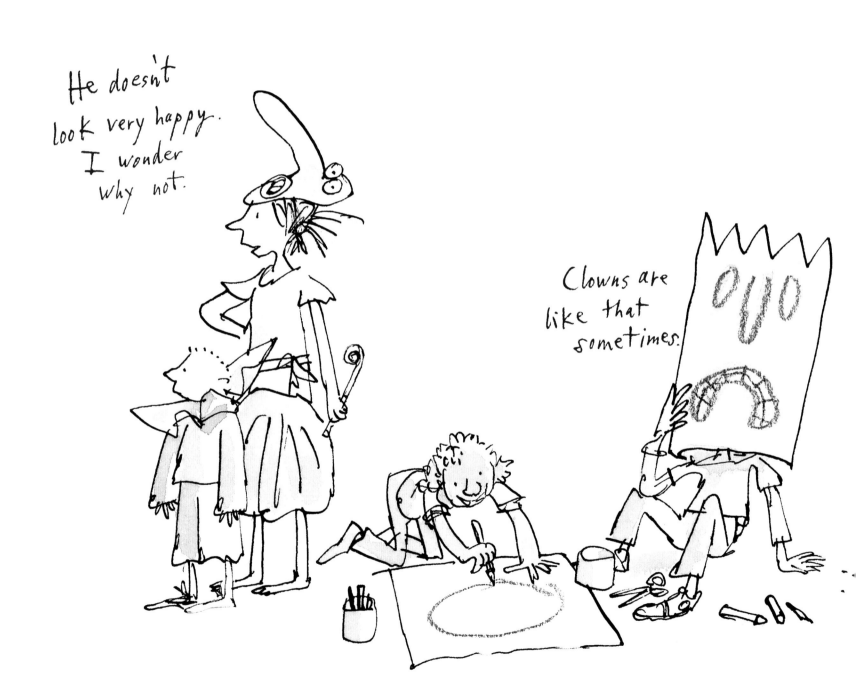

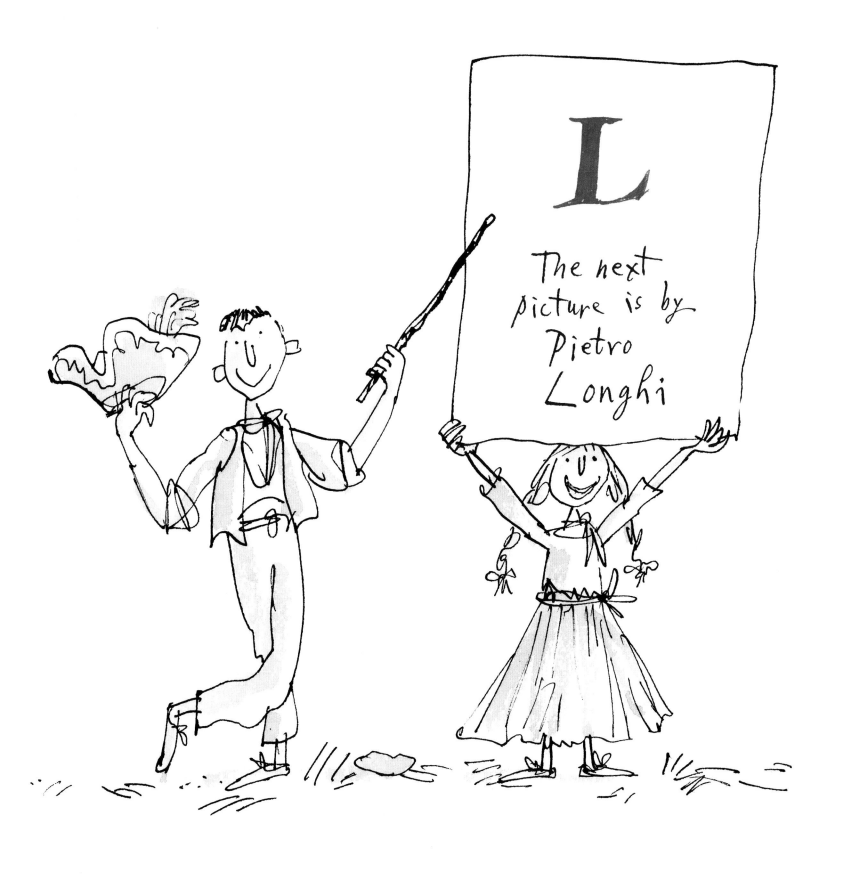

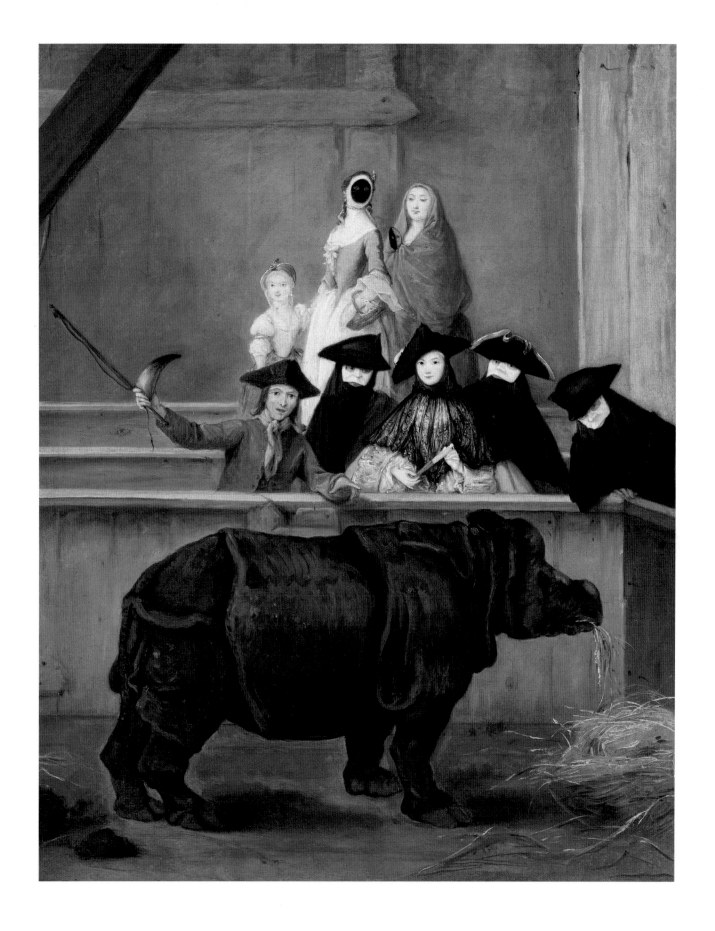

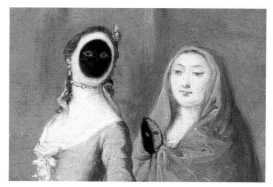

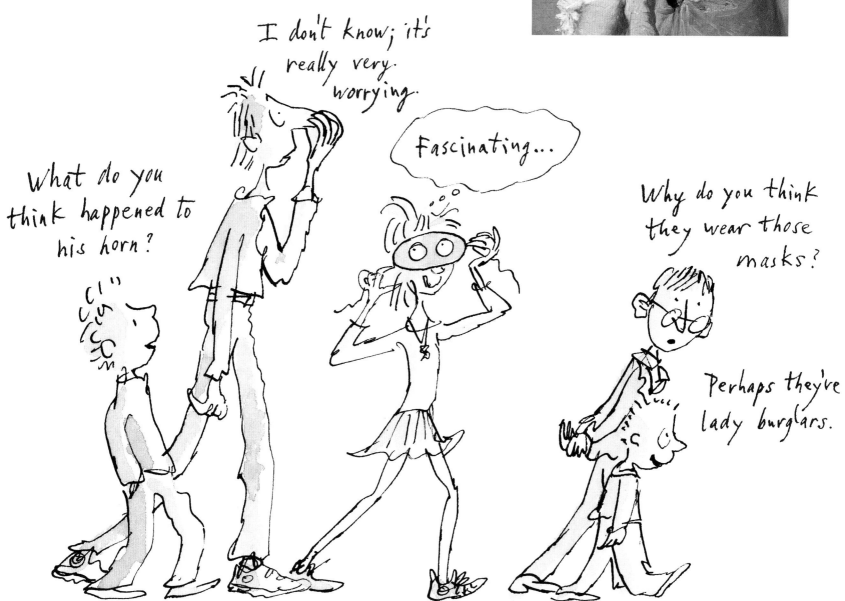

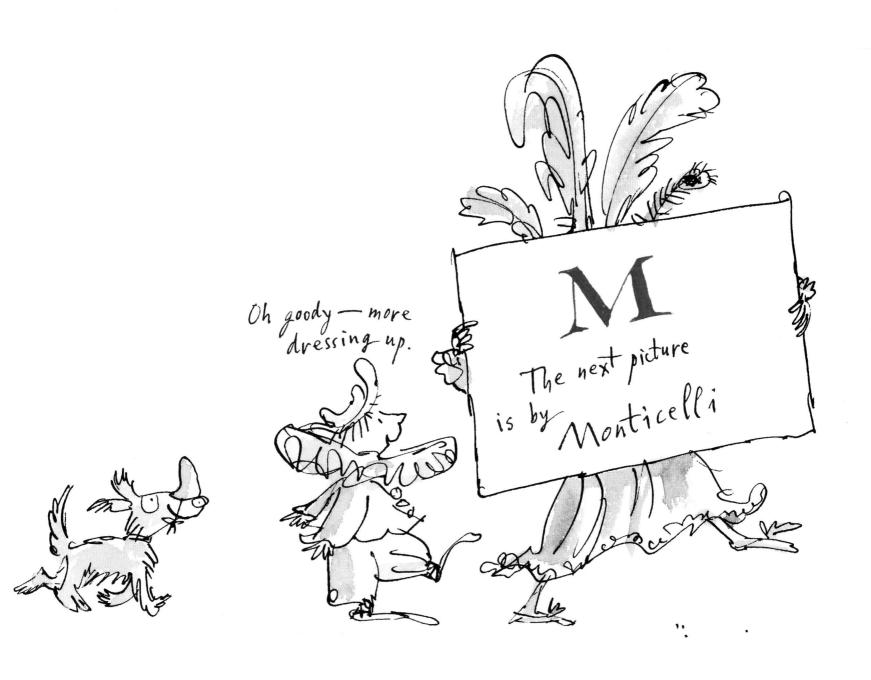

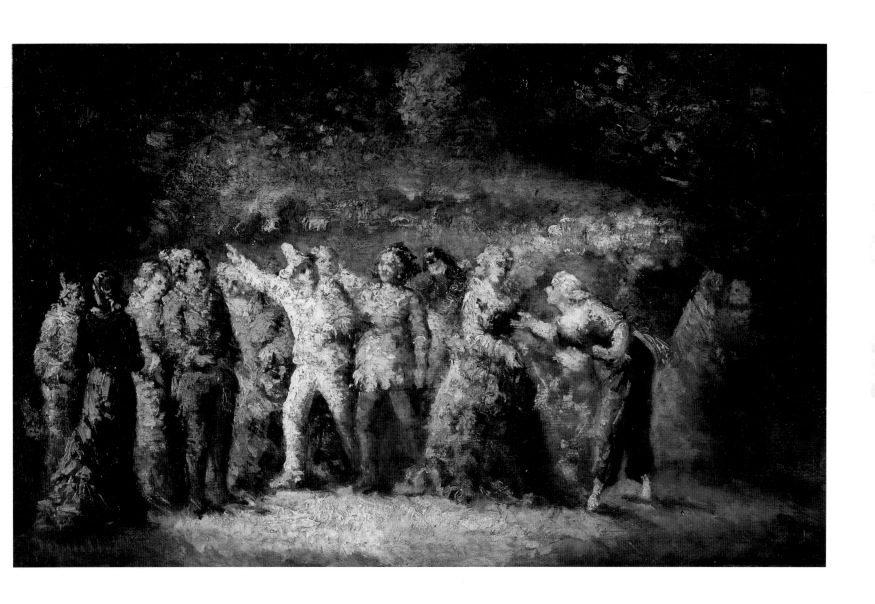

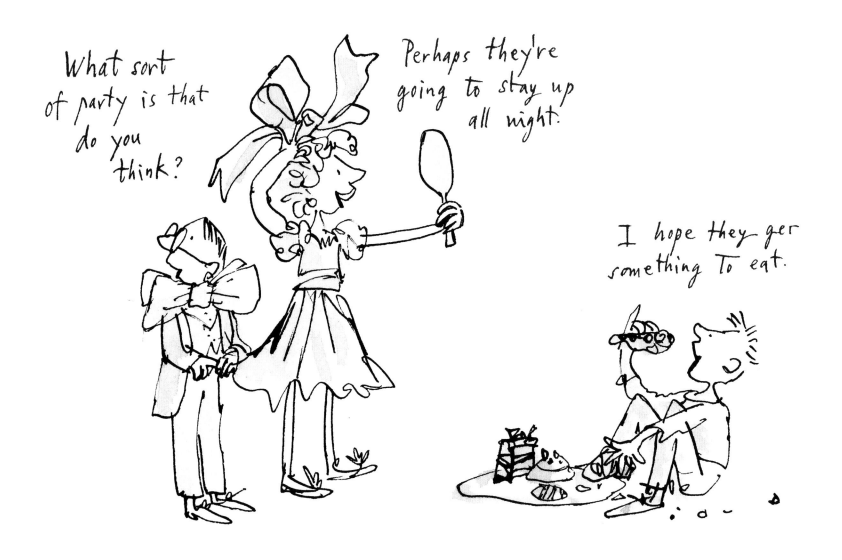

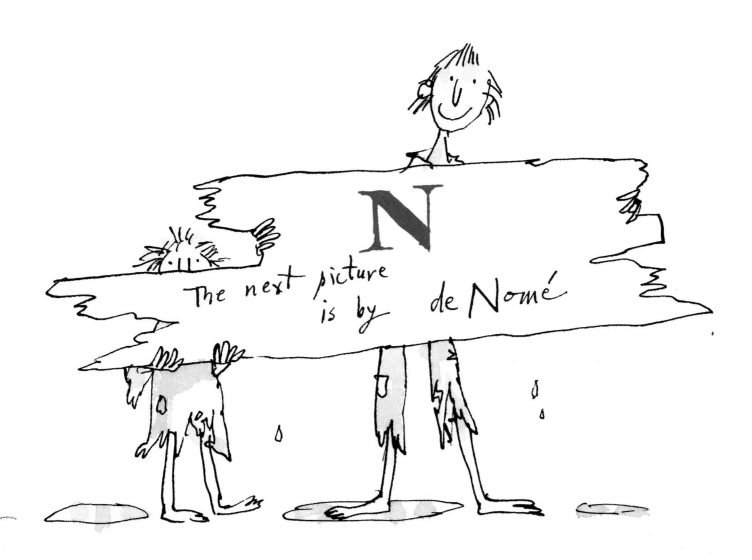

The next picture is by   de Nomé

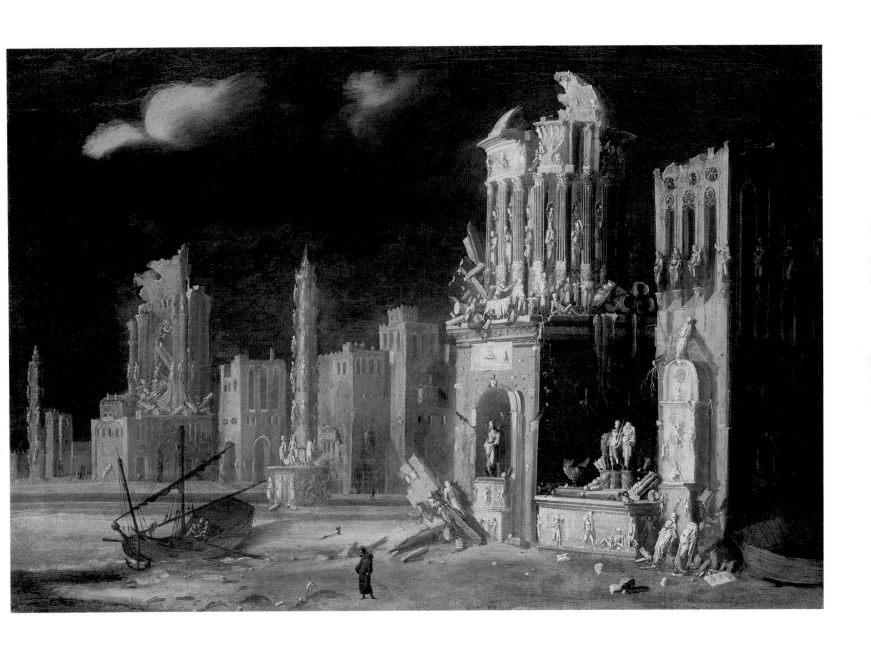

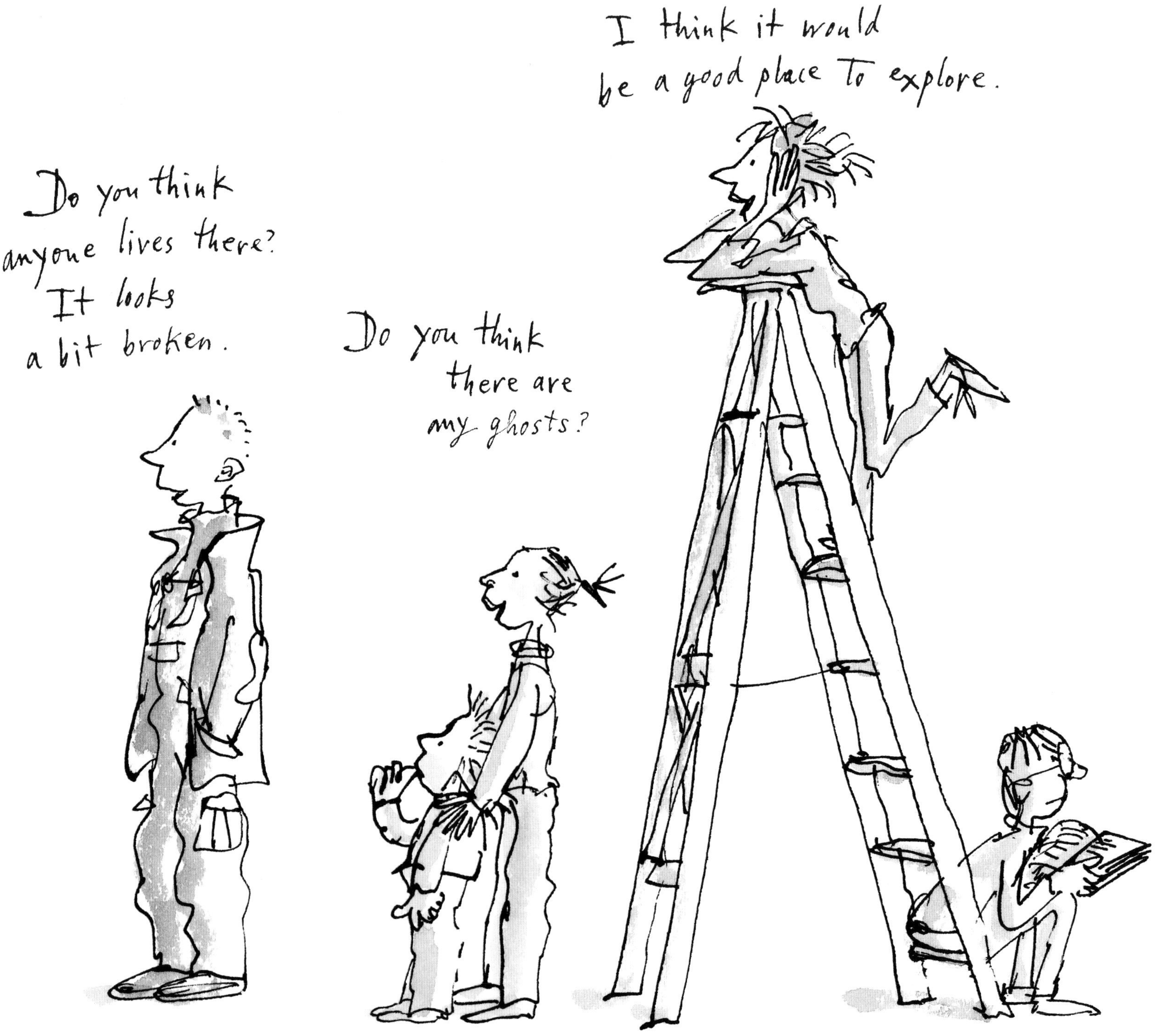
Do you think anyone lives there? It looks a bit broken.
Do you think there are any ghosts?
I think it would be a good place to explore.

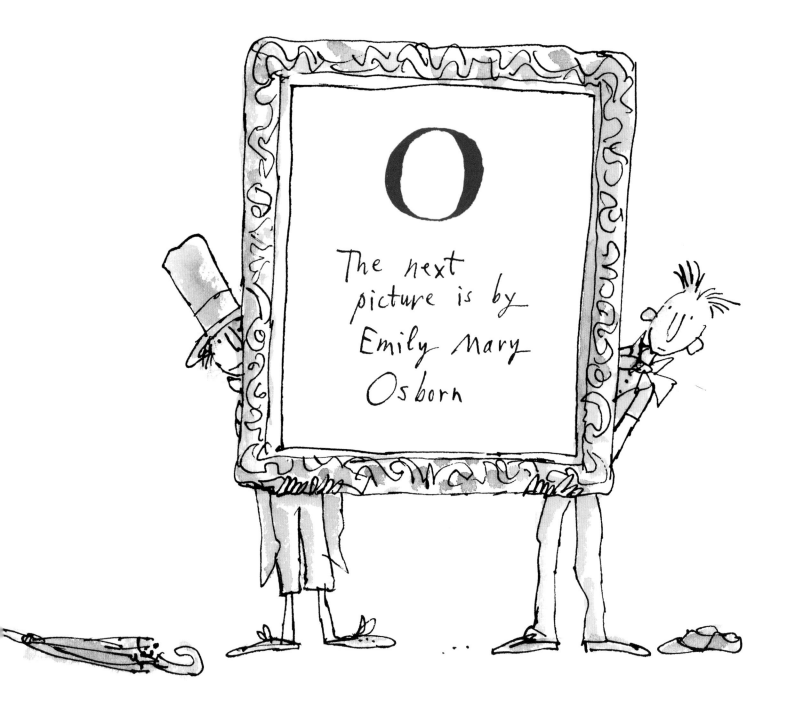

O

The next picture is by Emily Mary Osborn

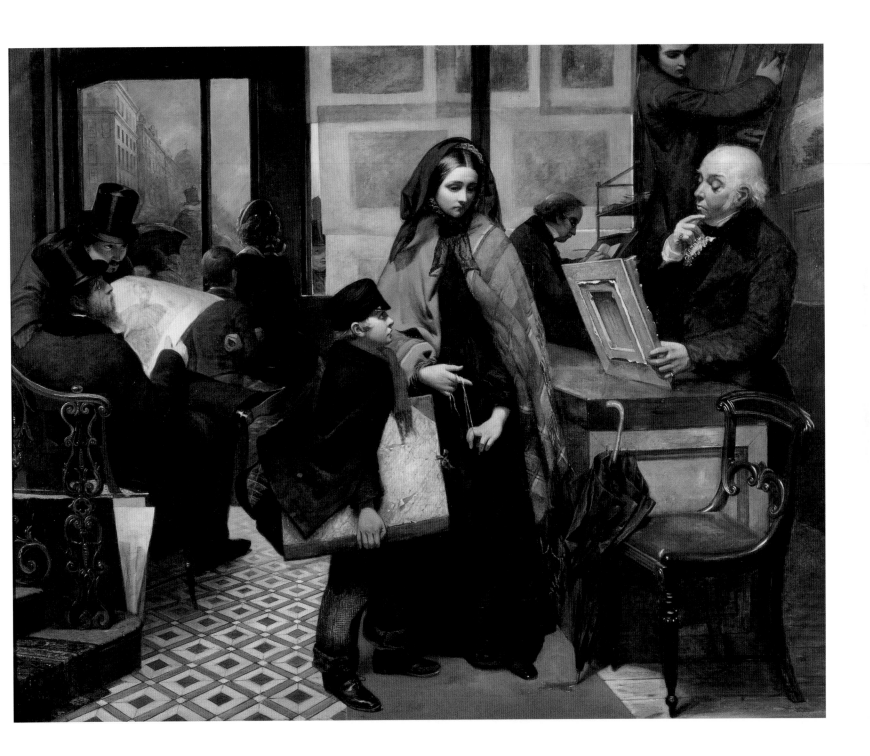

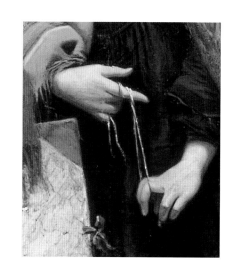

She does look rather sad.
I wonder what the picture is.

Nobody would buy <u>that</u>.

Do you think
he's going to buy it?

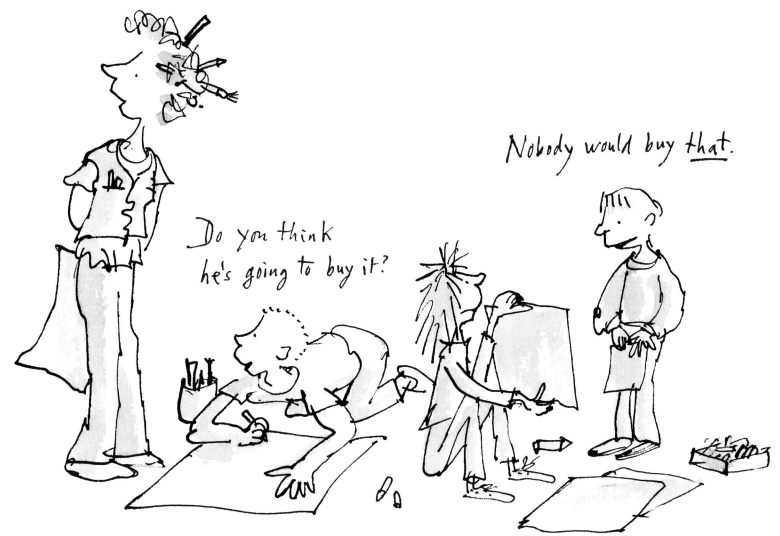

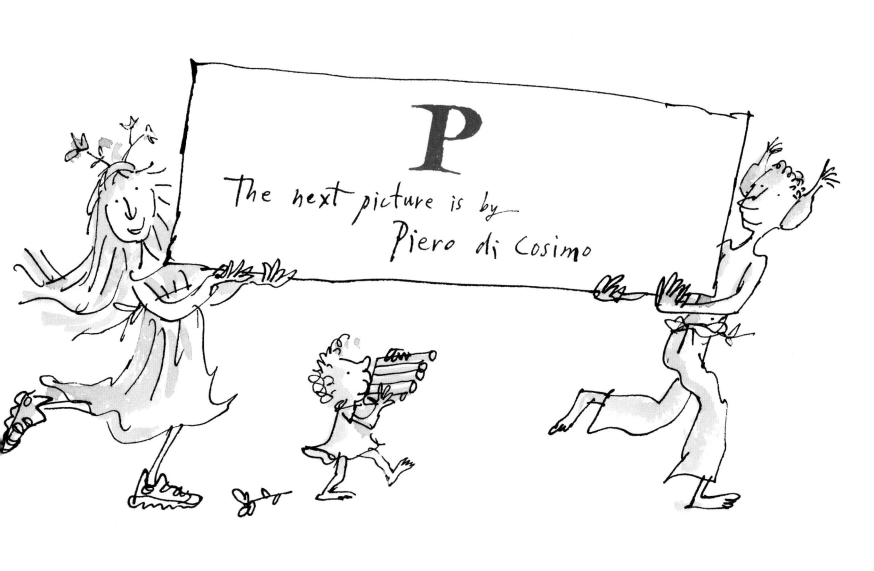

P

The next picture is by
Piero di Cosimo

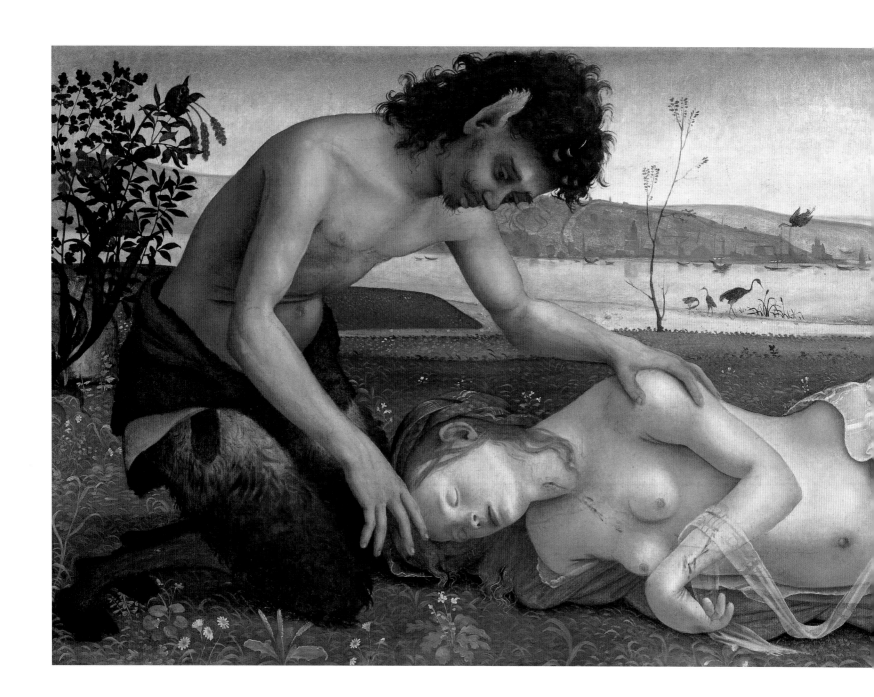

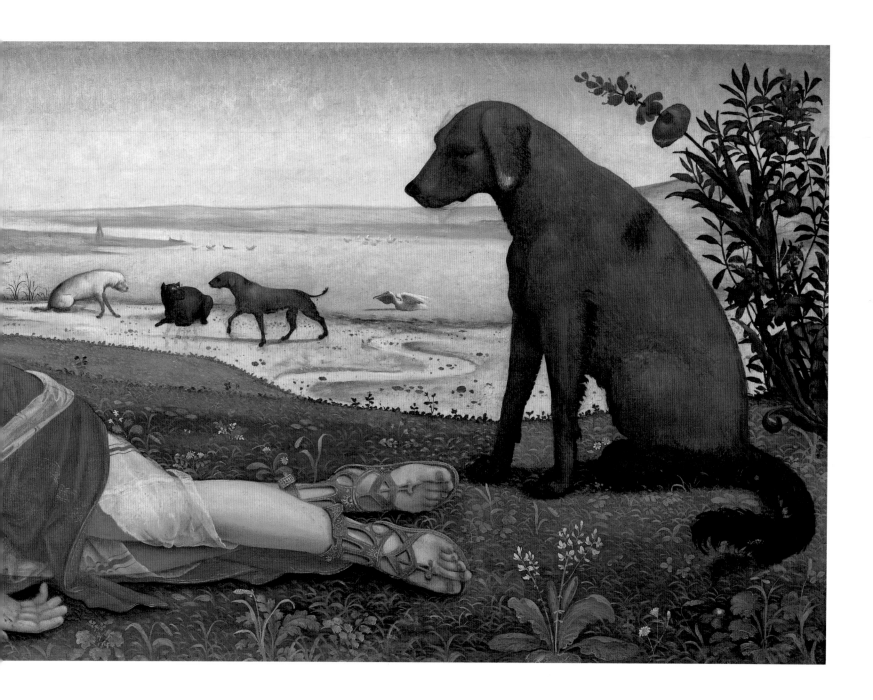

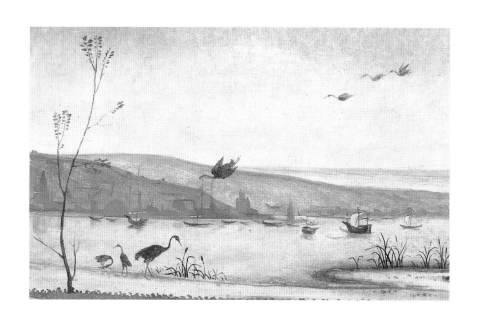

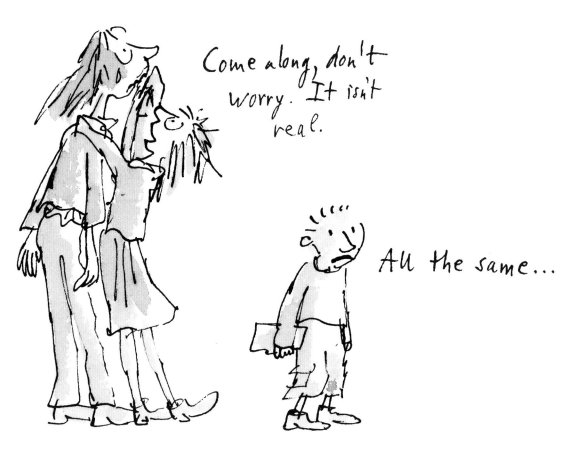

Come along, don't worry. It isn't real.

All the same...

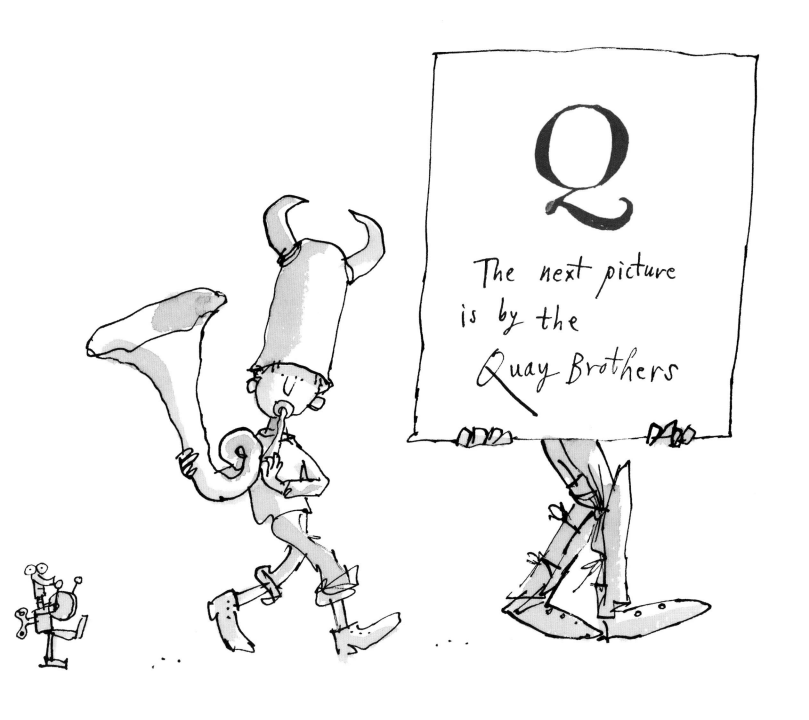

Q

The next picture
is by the
Quay Brothers

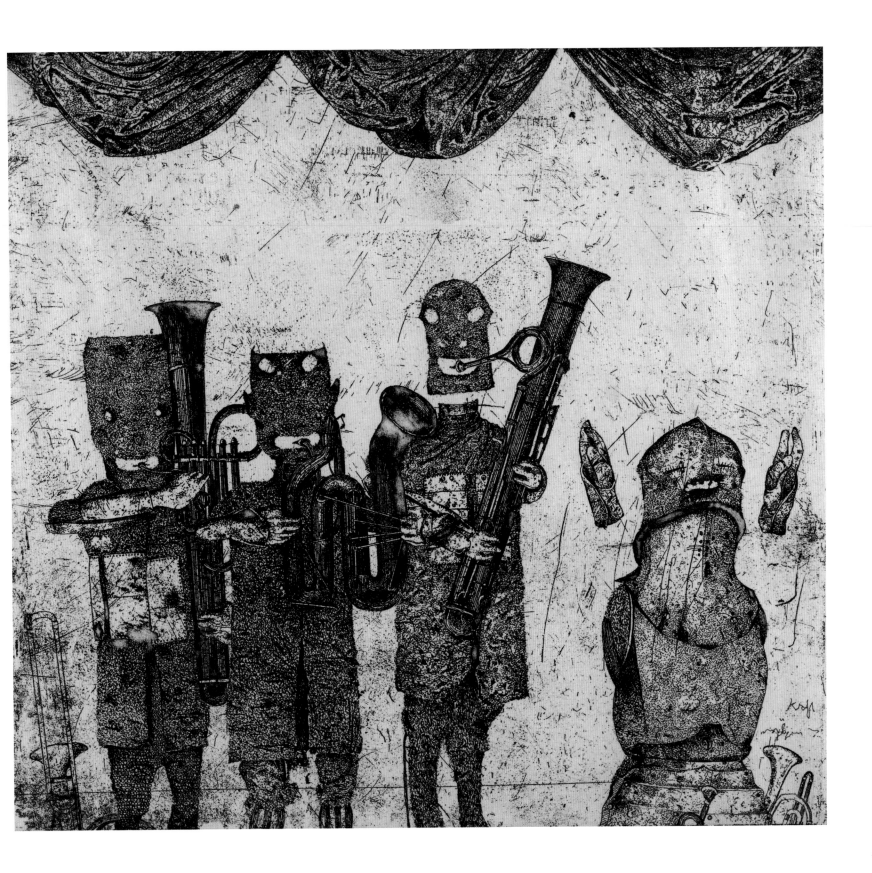

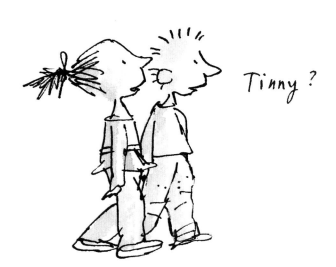

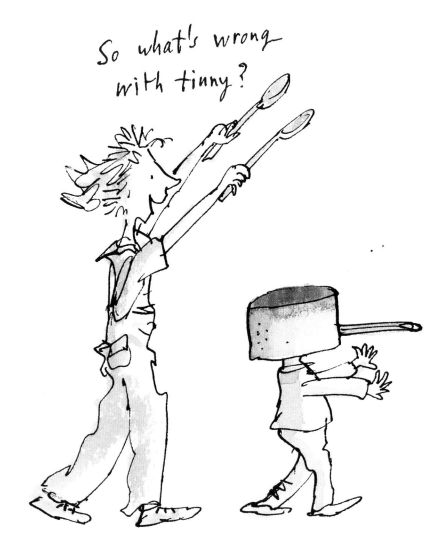

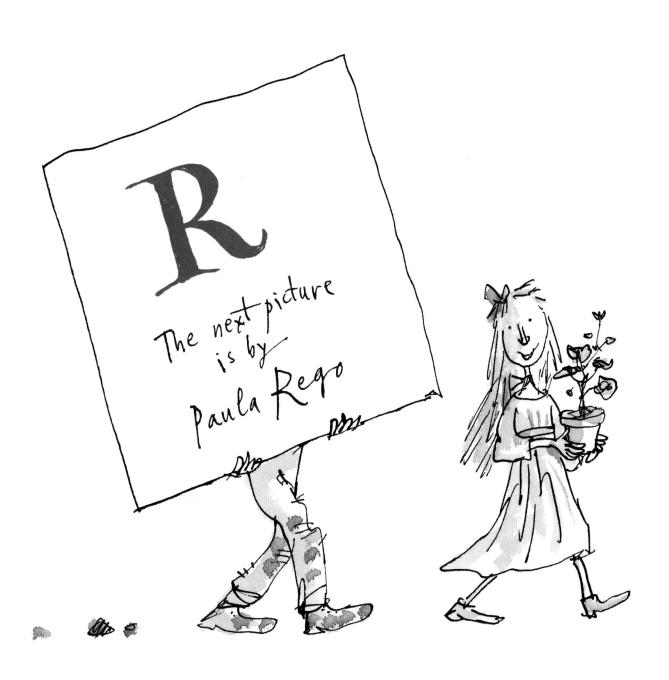

R

The next picture
is by
Paula Rego

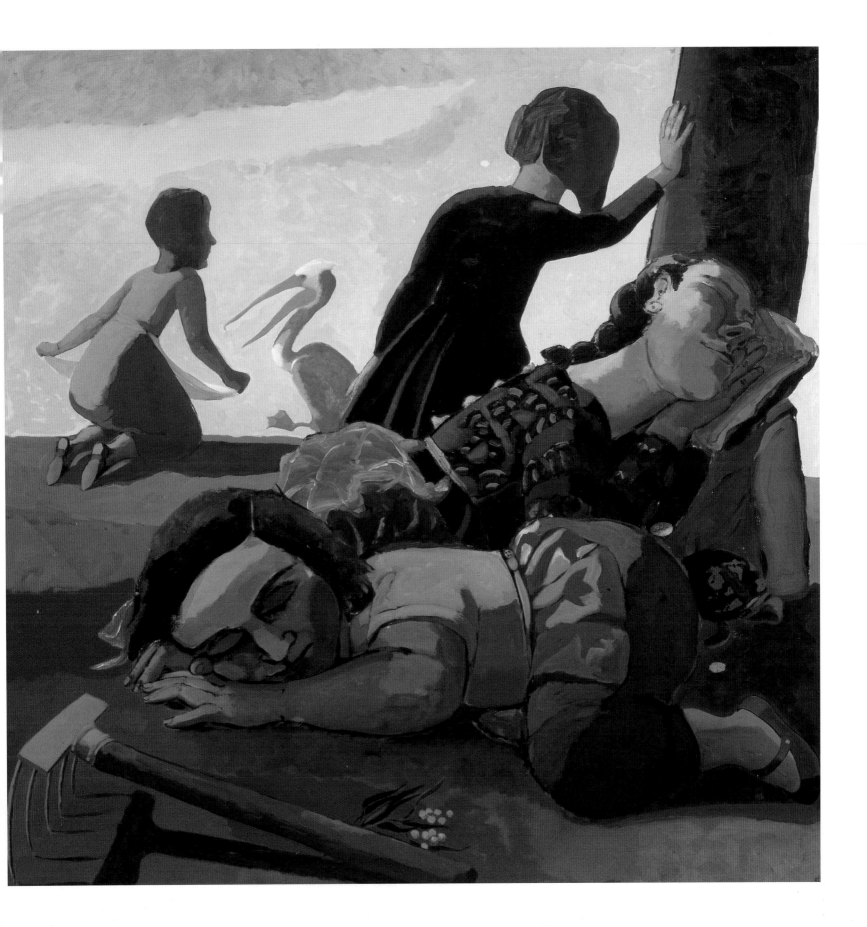

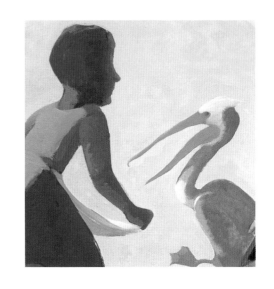

Why do
you think they're
asleep?

Sometimes
I do gardening
like that.

I think a
pelican is the
best bird in
the whole
world.

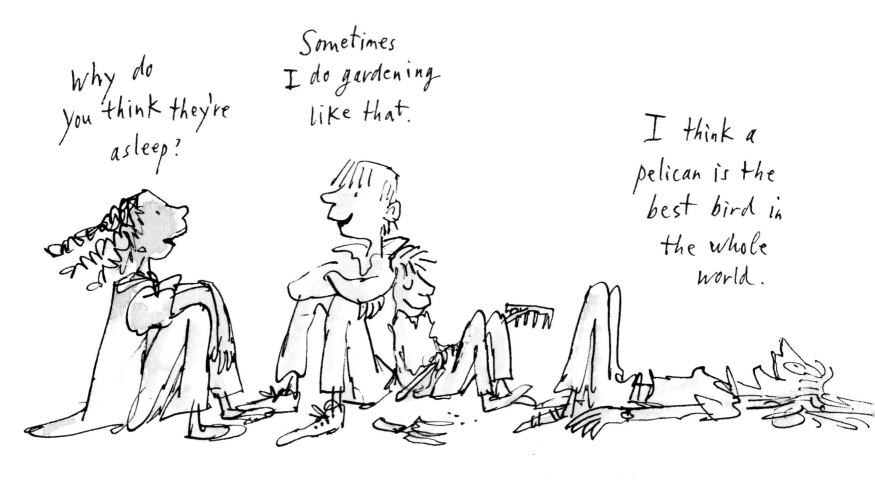

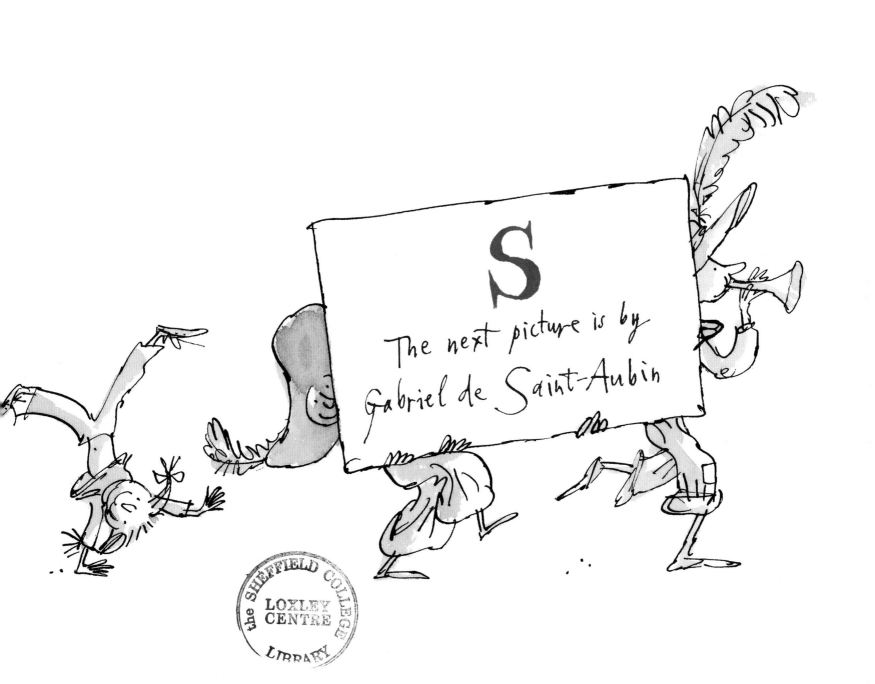

S

The next picture is by
Gabriel de Saint-Aubin

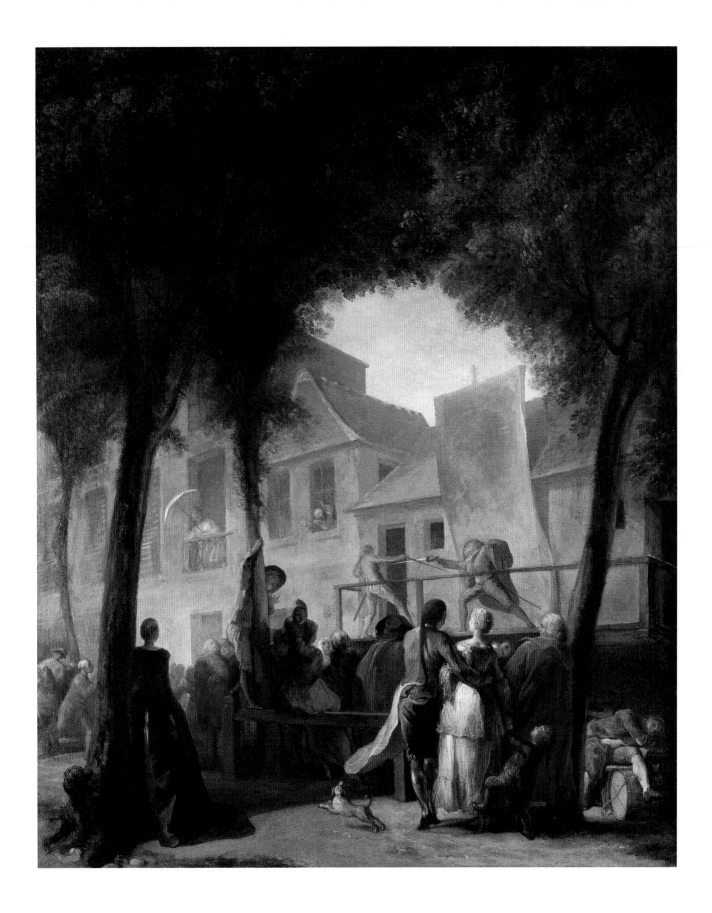

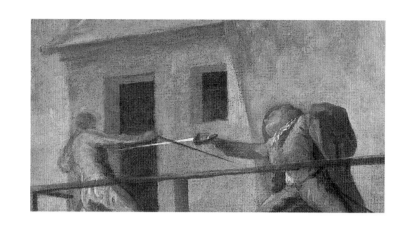

Is that a real fight or a sort of play?

We want one in front of our house.

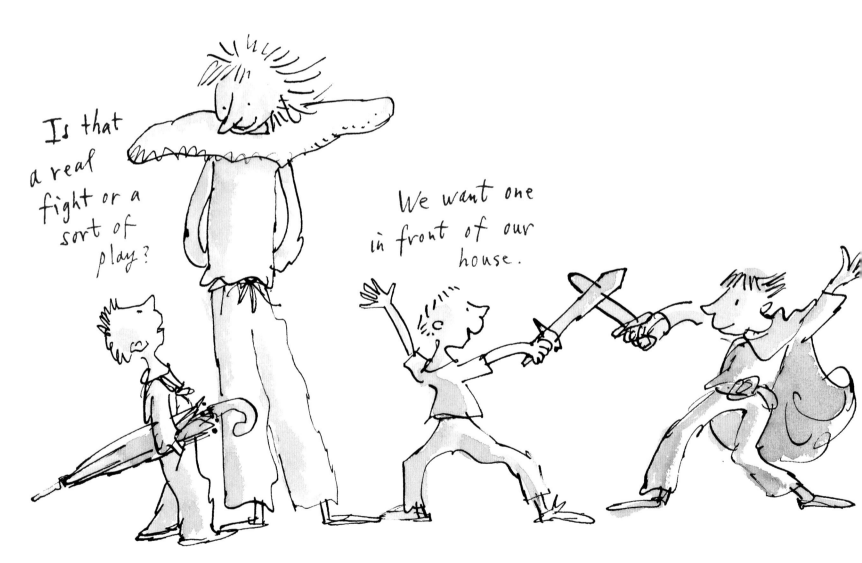

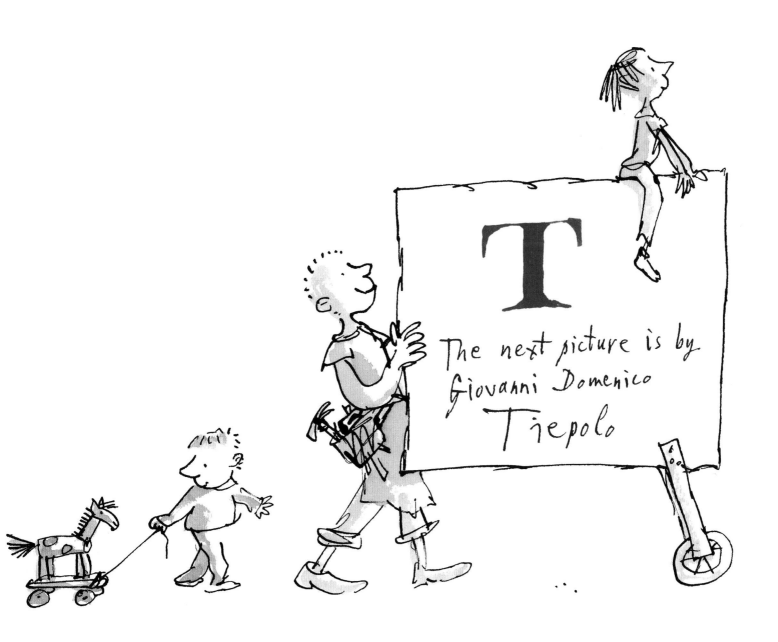

T

The next picture is by Giovanni Domenico Tiepolo

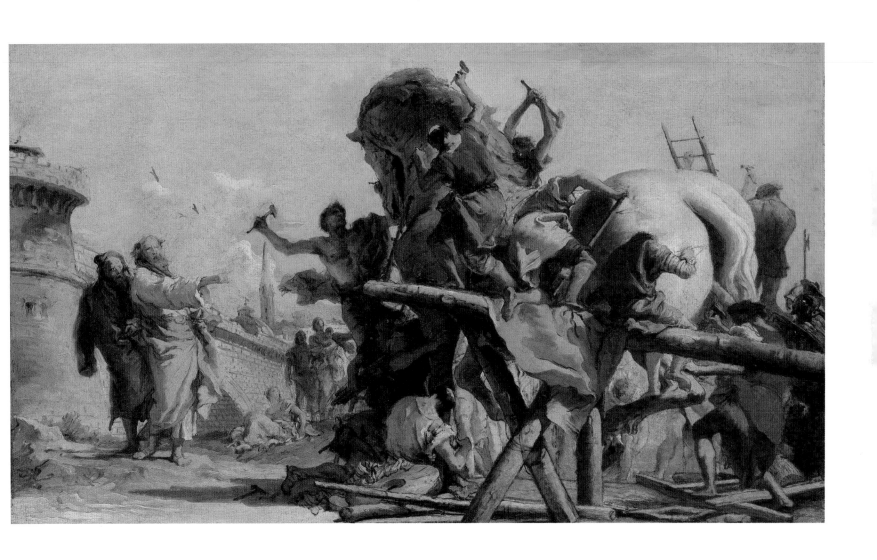

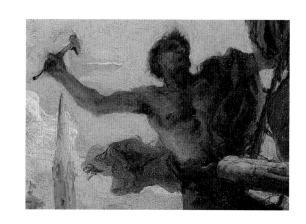

What a
lovely horse.

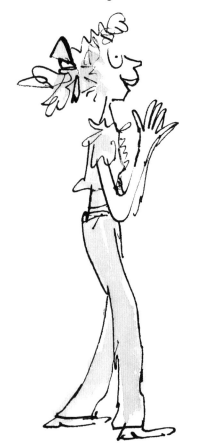

Are they building it
or are they
trying to
break it?

I think
it looks
fun.

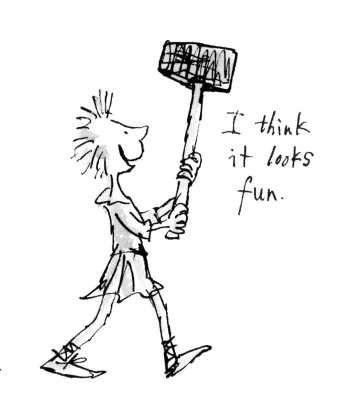

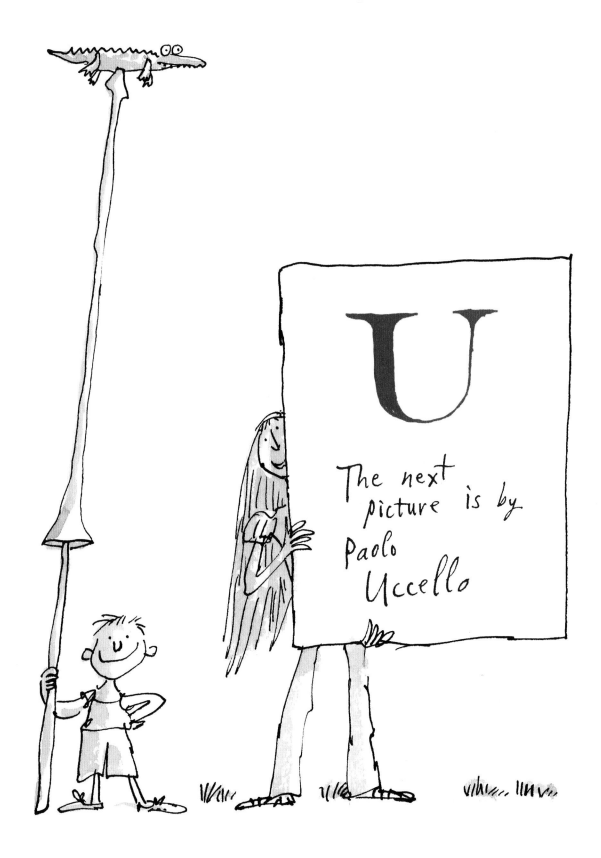

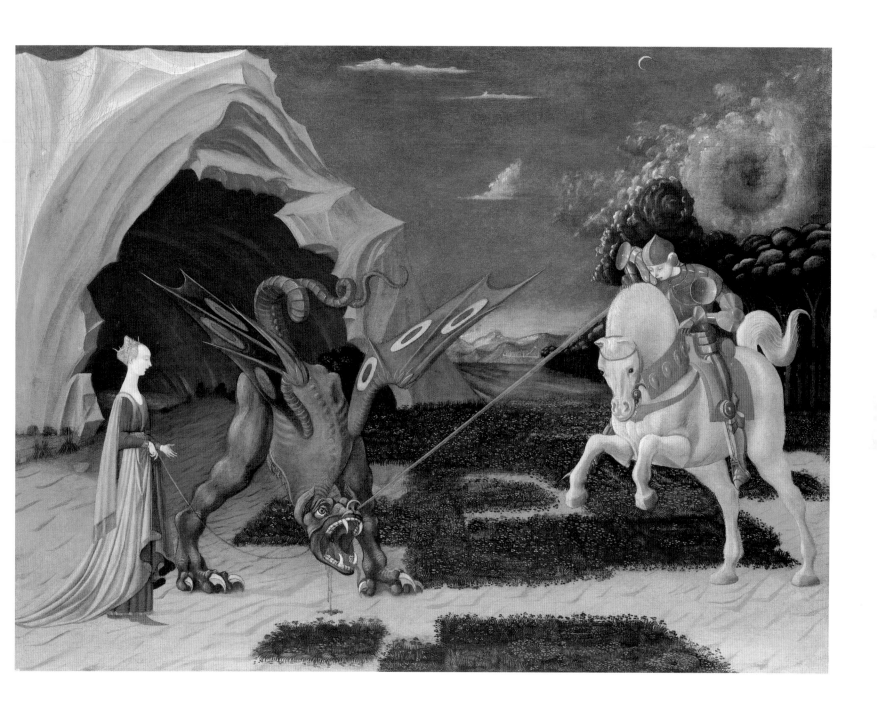

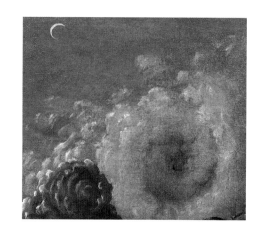

The lady
didn't look
very worried.

Well I feel
Sorry for
the dragon.
What had it
done to
deserve that?

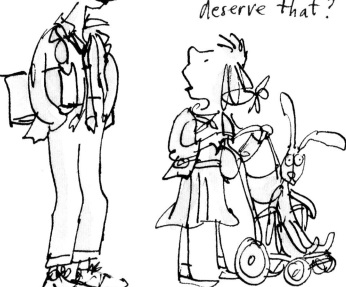

I don't think you
should treat anyone's
pet like that.

But did you
notice that
whirlwind

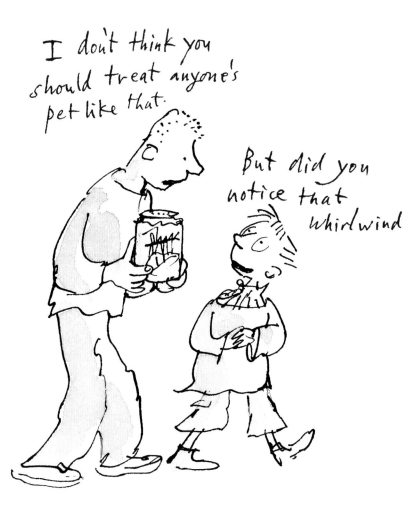

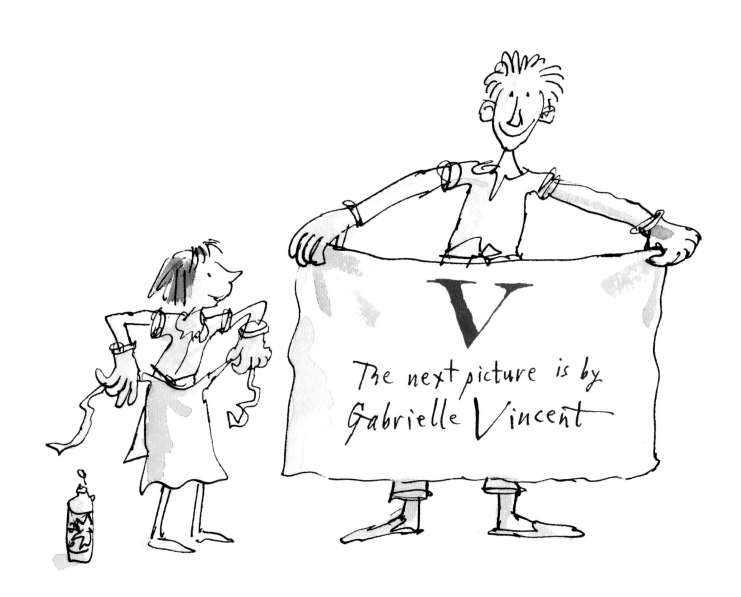

V

The next picture is by
Gabrielle Vincent

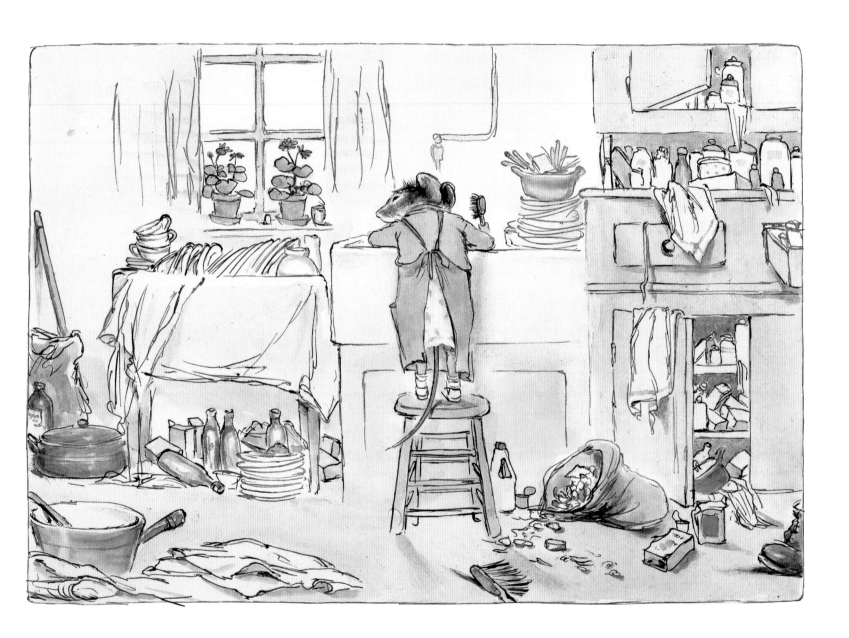

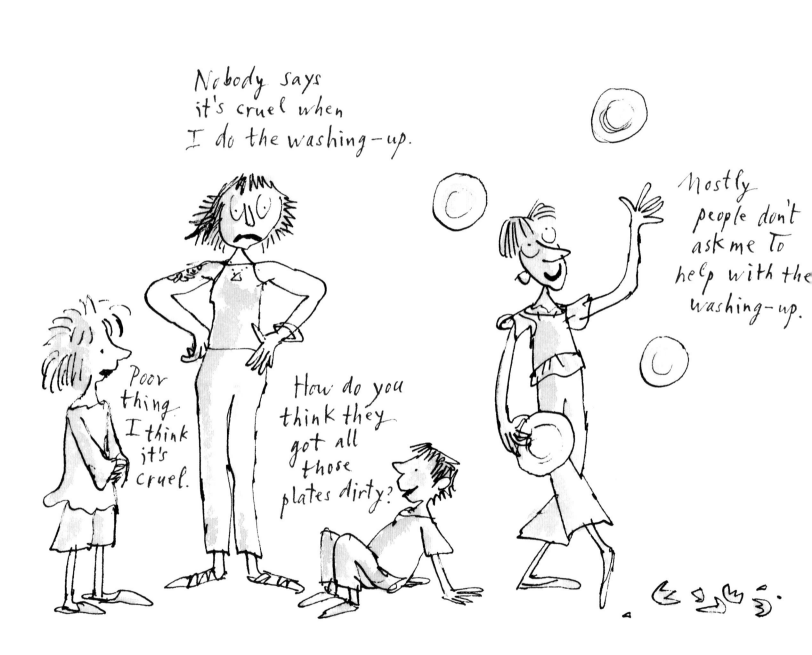

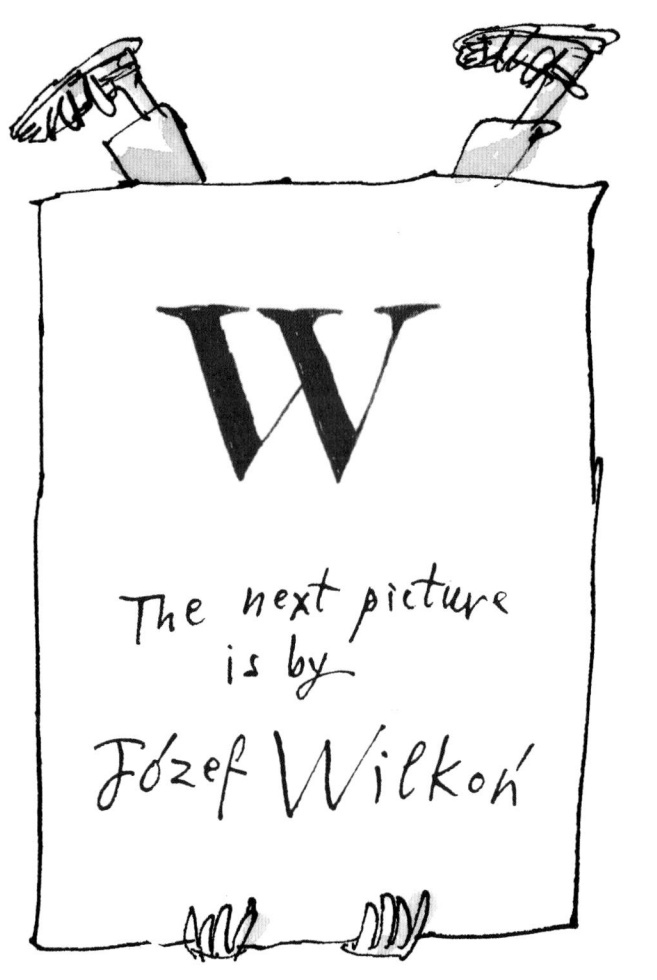

W

The next picture
is by

Józef Wilkoń

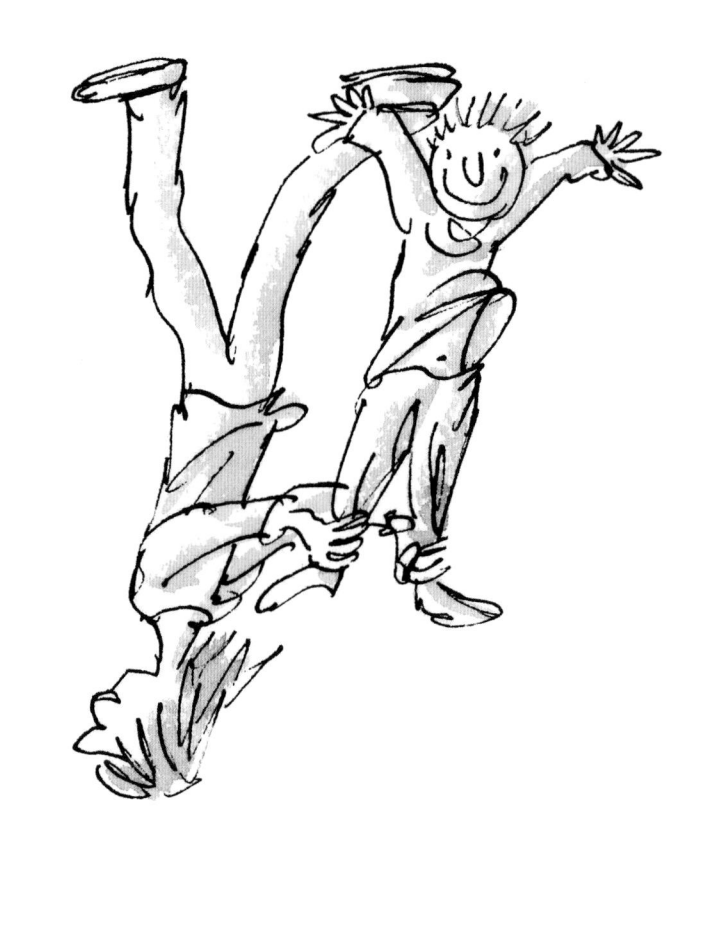

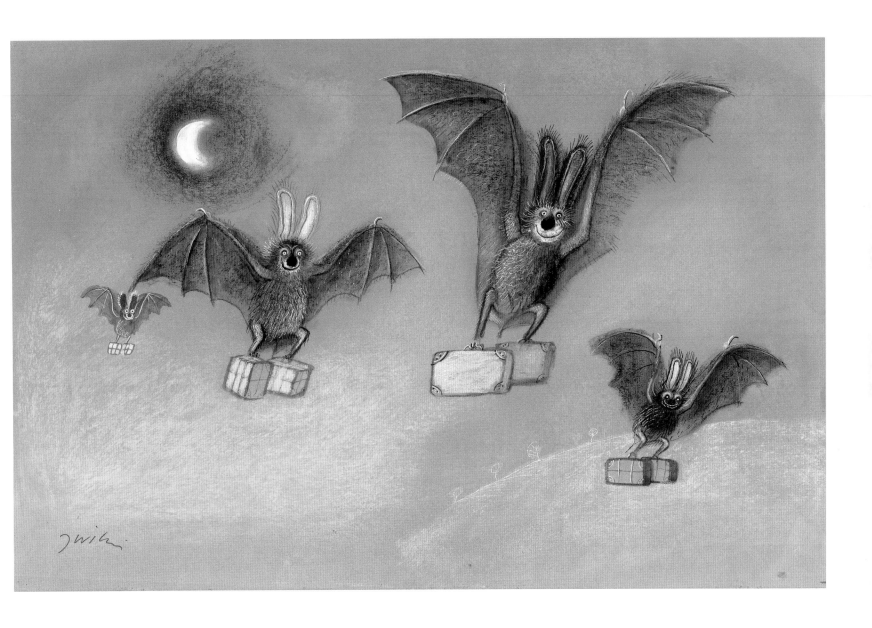

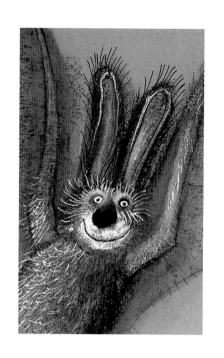

Are they going
on their holidays?

I'm not sure
animals have holidays.

Anyway,
we do.

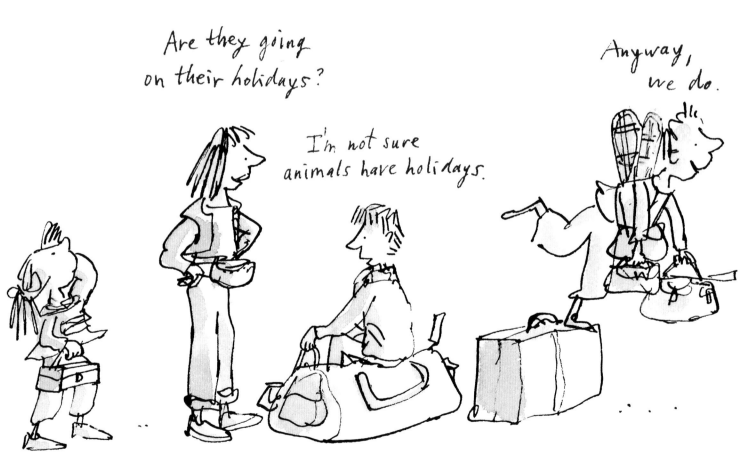

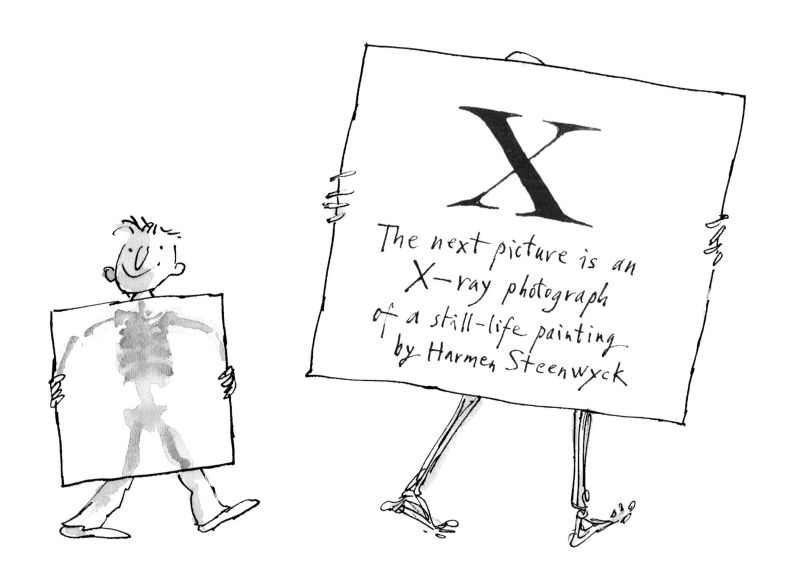

X

The next picture is an
X-ray photograph
of a still-life painting
by Harmen Steenwyck

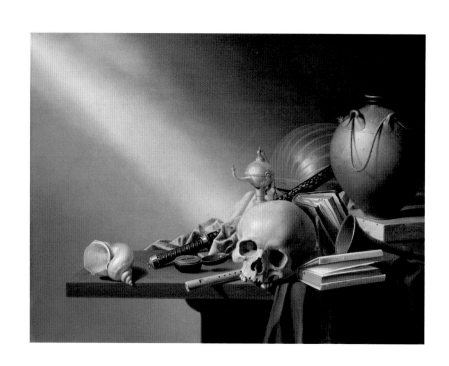

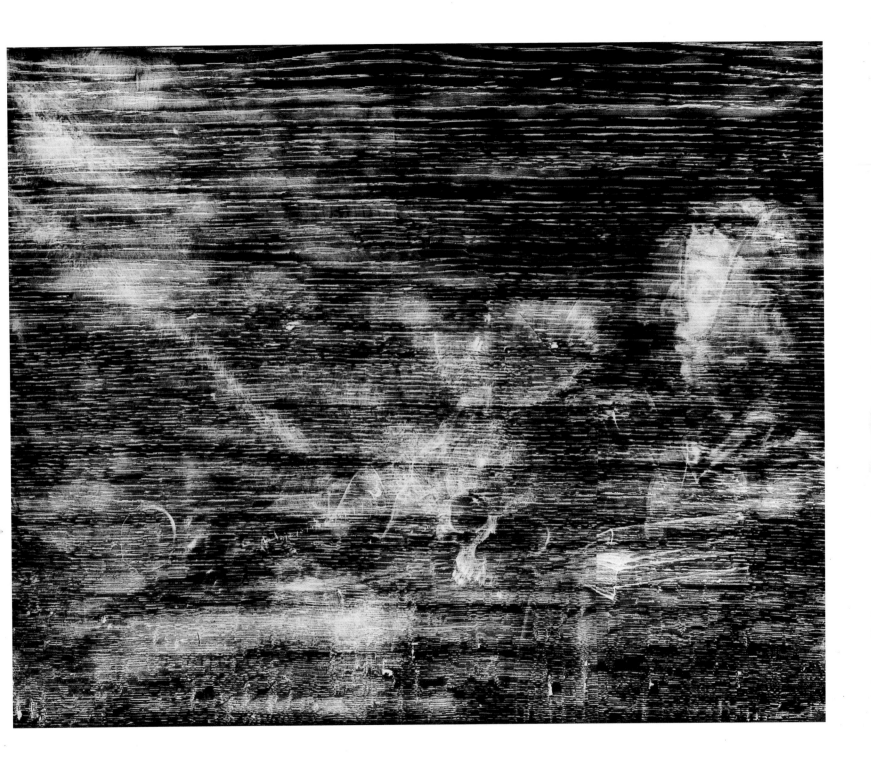

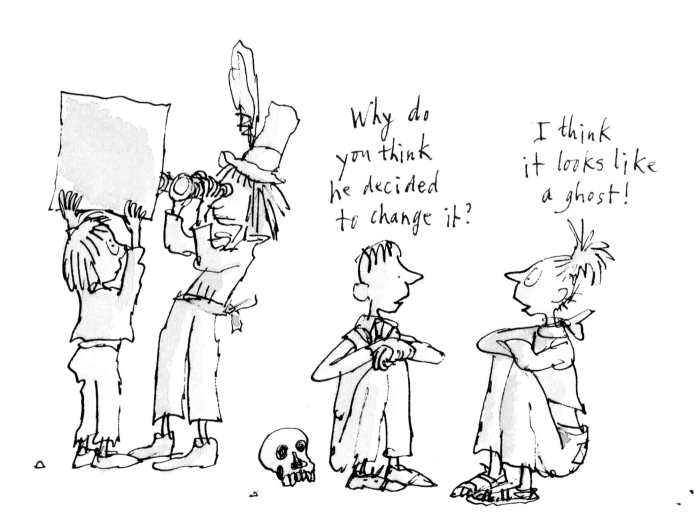

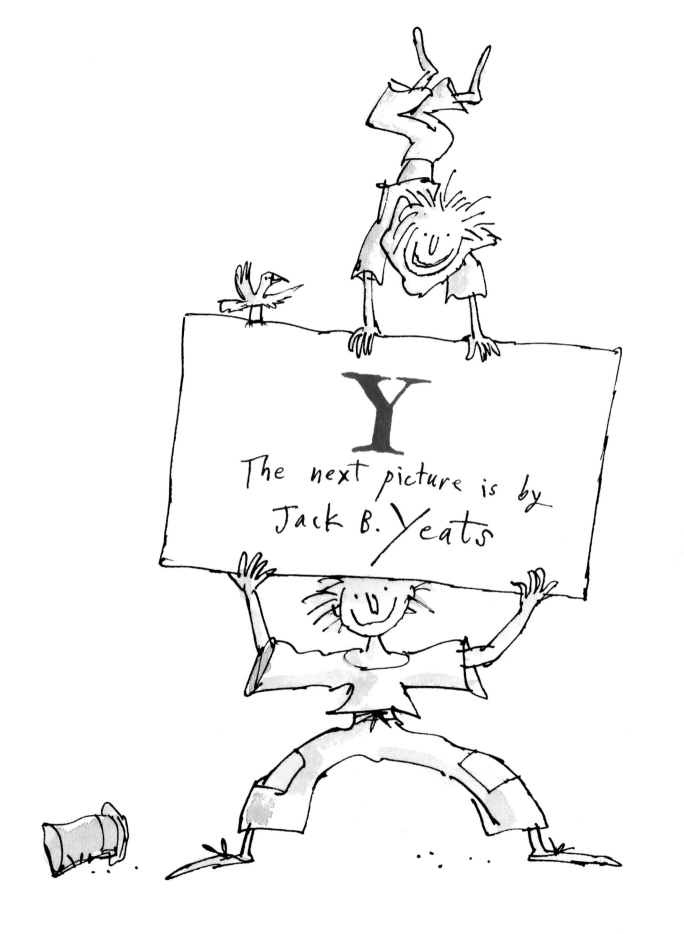

Y

The next picture is by
Jack B. Yeats

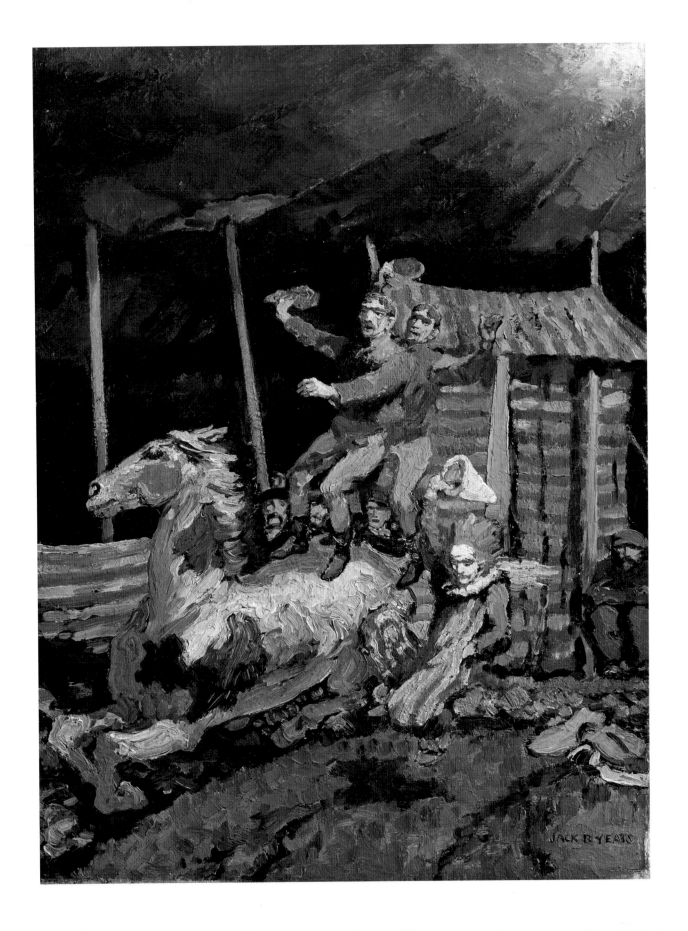

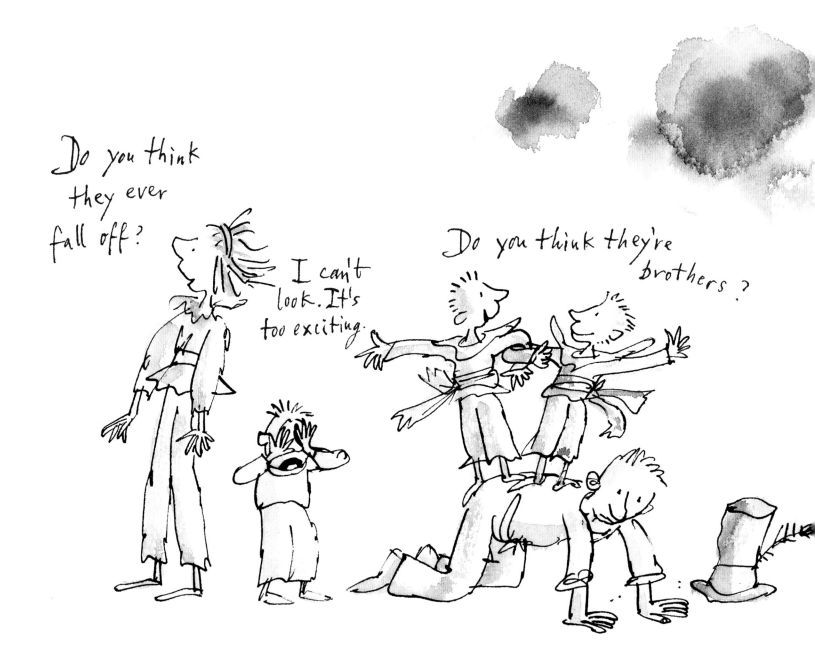

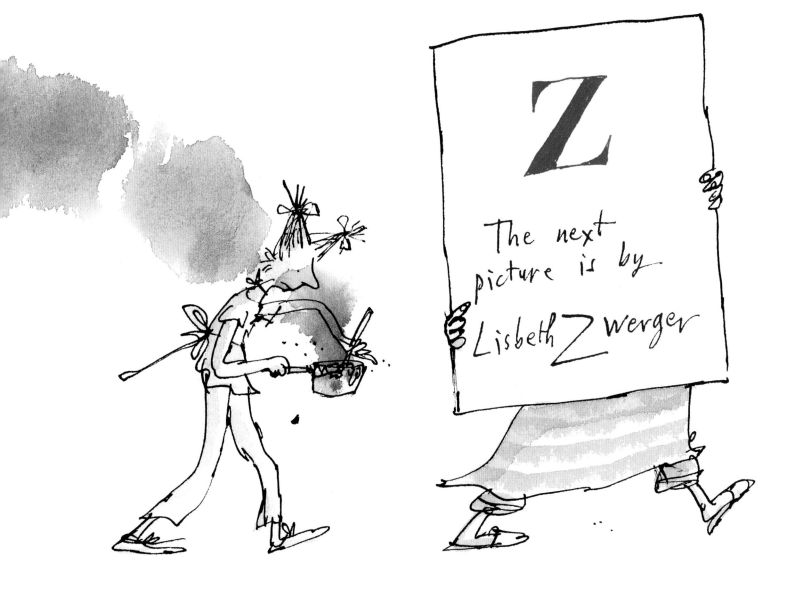

Z

The next picture is by Lisbeth Zwerger

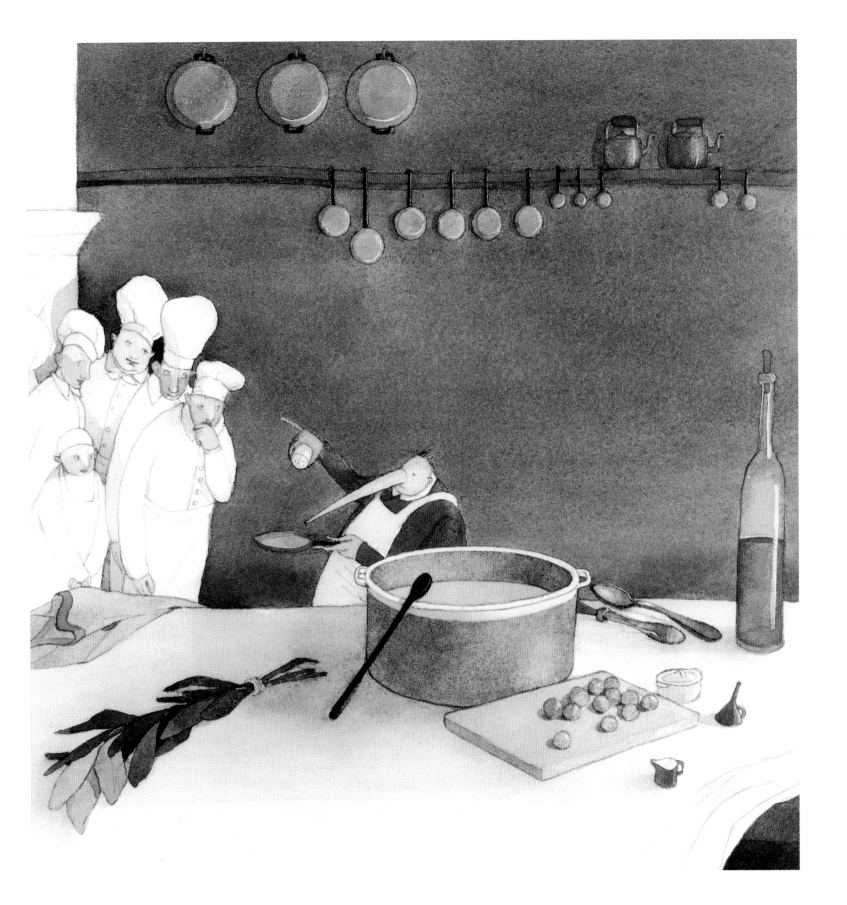

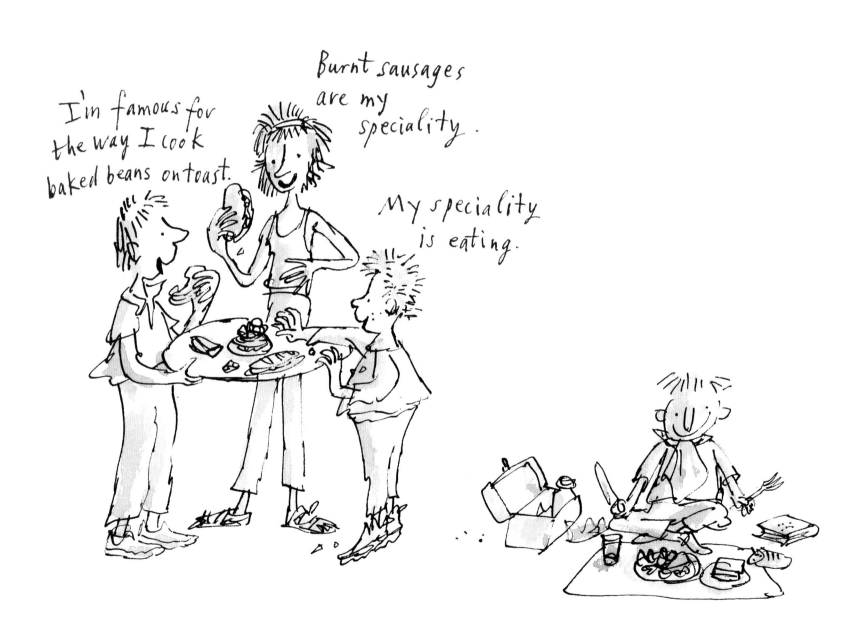

I think
he's seen enough
pictures
for today.

I'm going to
draw some
more!

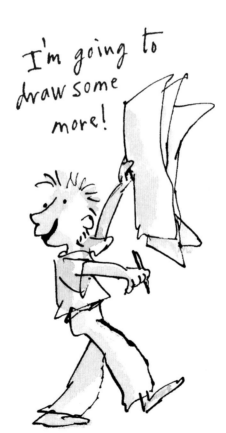
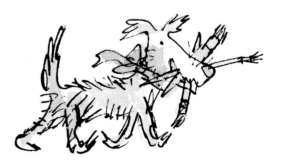

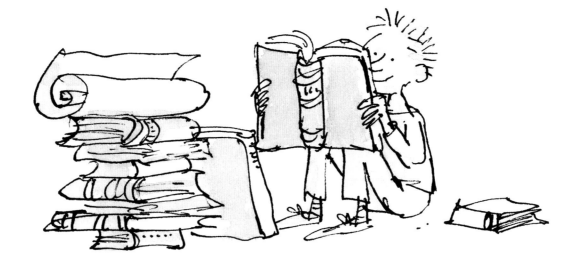

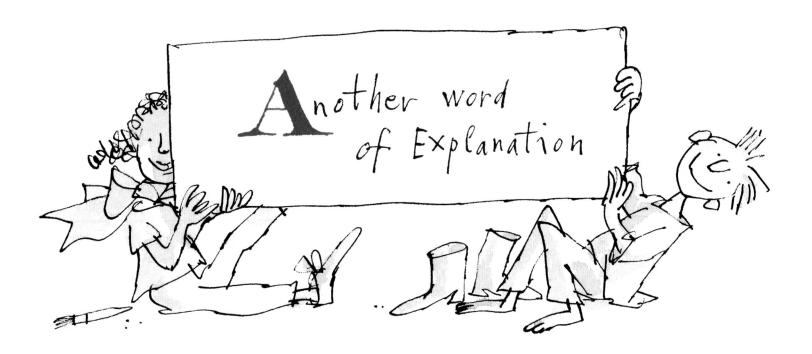

A s I mentioned at the beginning, the idea of this book is that you should look at each picture on its own and find out spontaneously what you feel about it, without being given any further information or commentary than the remarks of the young people who inhabit the intervening pages. However, if there are pictures in this book that you like, you may want to know more about them. The notes that follow will tell you something more about the pictures, where they come from and how they were painted. In addition they will tell you when the painters lived. Some of the artists in this book are alive and working now, but others lived at various times over the past 500 years, and in various countries.

This kind of knowledge can add to and enrich the way we look at pictures. However there is no doubt that what is most enriching is the experience of looking at real pictures. Then we respond immediately to their size, the way the paint is applied and the texture of their surfaces: the whole effect of their presence.

If you are someone who is setting off to visit a gallery with young people, there are one or two reminders that are perhaps worth repeating here. To begin with, don't feel obliged to 'do' all, or even as much as possible, of a gallery: it's too exhausting to the spirit and the legs. To settle on even two or three pictures, to look at them carefully while discussing what you see and feel, can often be quite enough. It also makes sense not to presume too quickly what is going to interest children: it's possible that a picture of another child may be less interesting than one of someone having their head cut off! Their choices can be surprising, and a picture they feel they have found alone can have a special value.

The whole idea of this book is to allow the viewers to have their personal reactions to a picture before discussing it further or giving more information. Similarly, even if you already know a lot about the paintings you are looking at in the gallery, it's better if you can elicit the children's own remarks and enquiries, rather than present a commentary – unless that is in fact what they are eager for.

I should also point out what's distinctive about illustration. You don't expect to see the originals of illustrations very often, although it's perfectly possible to talk about them in the same way as paintings, which is why some are included in this book. However, you do normally expect to see them in sequence in a book, where they are designed to go together and help each other tell a story. There is a lot to say about how these illustrations are produced, their effects and what we like about them. In the notes you will find the titles of the books that the illustrations shown here come from, as well as others by the same artists.

Keep on looking!

Quentin Blake

Hendrick Avercamp (1585–1634)

A Winter Scene with Skaters near a Castle

Painted in about 1608/9, measures 40.7 cm in diameter

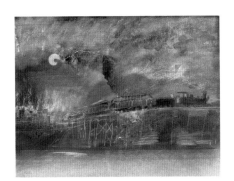

This painting is full of small stories. Among the people out on the ice, look out for a man begging, a couple colliding and another man fixing a woman's ice-skate. The castle is an imaginary one, but the Dutch flag flying on the boat moored next to it tells us that this is Holland. Avercamp signed the painting with his initials under the icy tree stump in the middle of the picture.

We do not know very much about Hendrick Avercamp. He was born in Amsterdam, but spent most of his life in the town of Kampen in the northern Netherlands. He was known as 'the mute of Kampen' because he could not speak, perhaps because he was also deaf. He painted busy winter scenes and made coloured drawings of people he might have come across in everyday life, such as farmers and fishermen.

John Burningham (1936–)

From *Oi! Get off our Train*

Published in 1989

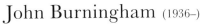

In this dramatic picture a small boy and a dog drive a steam train along a wooden viaduct over water. Under a cloudy moonlit sky they leave the city behind at the start of a dream-like adventure.

John Burningham is one of the best-known and most highly regarded of present day British illustrators. His work is full of sympathetic humour, while an experimental use of mixed media allows him to create strikingly atmospheric landscapes, as in this illustration from *Oi! Get off our Train*, a book commissioned by the Great Western Railway of Japan. His other books include *Harvey Slumfenburger's Christmas Present* and *Whaddayamean*.

Emma Chichester Clark (1954–)

A Love Affair

Painted in 1997, measures 160 x 220 cm

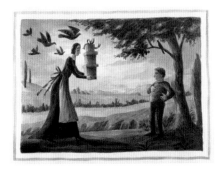

The tall figure of a young woman offers a heap of presents to a boy. Perhaps suprisingly, he seems reluctant to accept them. Instead he leans against the tree holding a cigar and looking up suspiciously. Birds seem to echo the characters' contrasting poses.

Emma Chichester Clark studied in London at the Chelsea School of Art and the Royal College of Art. She began her career as an illustrator of book jackets and as a gallery artist. More recently she has become best known as an illustrator of children's books, including titles of her own such as *More!* and *I Love You, Blue Kangaroo*. However, *A Love Affair* is not taken from a book.

Honoré-Victorin Daumier (1808–1879)
Don Quixote and Sancho Panza
Probably painted before 1866, measures 40.3 x 64.1 cm

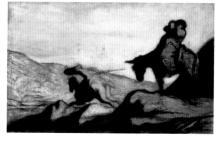

Don Quixote was an extraordinary knight who had some bizarre adventures, as told by the seventeenth-century Spanish author Miguel de Cervantes. Here, Don Quixote dramatically charges at a flock of sheep believing it to be the enemy. Meanwhile his servant Sancho Panza waits on his donkey. Perhaps he is taking time out for a drink, or maybe he is wringing his hands in despair at the knight's stupidity. This work is actually a preparatory sketch for a more finished painting.

Honoré-Victorin Daumier lived in Paris for almost all his life. He made his living illustrating satirical newspapers commenting on the political and social life of the time. He also painted scenes from literature and mythology.

Adam Elsheimer (1578–1610)
Saint Paul on Malta
Painted in about 1600, measures 16.8 x 21.3 cm

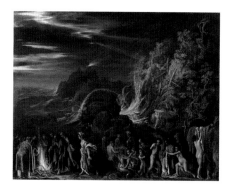

The Bible (Acts of the Apostles 28:2–6) tells the story of how a terrible storm shipwrecked Saint Paul, who in the picture is wearing a red-lined cloak, and his companions on the Mediterranean island of Malta. The islanders welcomed the sailors and lit fires to warm the survivors. However, as Paul threw sticks on to the fire a snake darted out and bit his hand. The islanders thought that this must be a divine punishment for some previous crime, but when Paul shook off the snake they saw he had not been hurt. The people then believed he was a god.

This picture is actually smaller than it appears in this book, but you can just make out the stormy sea and scattered wreck of the ship in the background. In the foreground survivors huddle around fires and hang out their wet clothes to dry.

Adam Elsheimer was born in Germany but settled in Rome where he became especially famous for his night landscapes.

Michael Foreman (1938–)
From *Seasons of Splendour*
Published in 1985

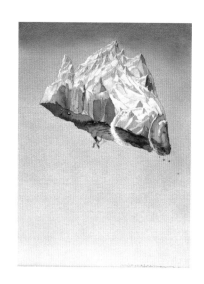

This picture is an illustration from *Seasons of Splendour*, a book of Indian folk tales collected by Madhur Jaffrey. The monkey Hanuman is on a mission to the Himalayas in search of special healing herbs to revive the prince-god Ram's wounded army. The monkey arrives at the mountains at nightfall and is unable to distinguish one plant from another. Rather than pick the wrong herb, he decides to take the whole mountain to the army instead.

Michael Foreman was born in Lowestoft and studied at St Martin's School of Art and the Royal College of Art in London. His work is marked by its humour and draughtsmanship which combine with his imaginative sense of fantasy to make him one of the best contemporary illustrators of folk and fairy tales. Among his books are *Peter Pan and Wendy* and *The Shining Princess and other Japanese Legends*.

Francisco de Goya (1746–1828)
A Scene from El Hechizado por Fuerza ('The Forcibly Bewitched')
Painted in 1798, measures 42.5 x 30.8 cm

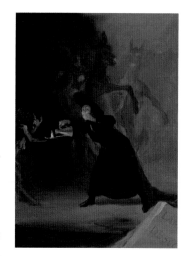

This scene is from a seventeenth-century Spanish comic play by Antonio de Zamora. Doña Leonora wants to marry the timid and gullible Don Claudio, but he resists until she frightens him with a trick. She makes him believe that her slave Lucía has bewitched him, and that he will only stay alive if the lamp in Lucía's room is kept alight. He is shown pouring oil into a lamp shaped like a ram. In the play he calls the lamp a 'monstrous' one ('lampara descomunal') and you can read the first parts of these two words on the right. A grotesque painting of dancing donkeys, just visible on the wall behind him, has added to his terror.

Francisco de Goya was one of the most famous and admired Spanish painters. He became painter to the King of Spain in 1786, but he moved to Bordeaux in 1824 after suffering from a serious illness which made him deaf. During his long life he made many etchings, as well as painting a large number of portraits and subject pictures.

Edward Hopper (1882–1967)
Night in the Park
Made in 1921, measures 17.8 x 21.3 cm

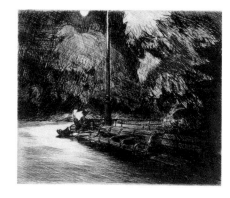

In this atmospheric picture a solitary man sits on a park bench reading a newspaper by the light of a street lamp. The scene is one of a set of etchings by the American artist Edward Hopper. They mainly show everyday aspects of contemporary American life in the city or countryside, often simple activities such as a man walking down a street, a woman looking out of a window, or children playing outside a house. The images are direct and straightforward, but their contrasts of light and shade and unusual perspectives make them strongly emotional.

Edward Hopper is one of America's most popular twentieth-century artists. He was born in New York State and studied commercial illustration and painting. He developed a style of composition involving flat masses of colour and large, simple geometric forms.

Roberto Innocenti (1940–)
From *The Adventures of Pinocchio*
Published in 1988

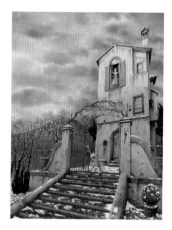

Pinocchio, the wooden puppet-hero, kneels before a house where a young woman appears at a high window. To the left of this wintry scene lurk two sinister cloaked figures.

    This work is an illustration to Carlo Collodi's classic Italian children's book *Pinocchio* in Roberto Innocenti's characteristic style: a combination of realistic detail and sombre atmosphere. He has illustrated many books including Charles Dickens's *A Christmas Carol*, Charles Perrault's *Cinderella*, E.T.A. Hoffman's *Nutcracker* and *Rose Blanche*, a book of his own about the experiences of a child under the Nazis. Innocenti was born near Florence in 1940. Although he had no professional art training he began designing books and theatre posters, before moving on to book illustration.

David Jones (1895–1974)
The Garden Enclosed
Painted in 1924, measures 35.6 x 29.8 cm

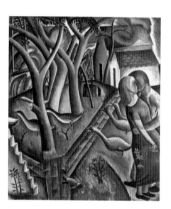

This picture shows two figures embracing, but we almost miss them as so much is going on around them: trees wave agitated branches and a flock of geese makes its way across the picture. A bright red path leads to a house in the background, there is a child's swing on the left and a doll lies discarded on the ground near the girl.

    David Jones painted this picture to mark his engagement to Petra Gill, daughter of the artist Eric Gill. The two figures are the artist and his new fiancée, who was not quite eighteen at the time. The doll may represent the childhood that Petra is now leaving behind.

    David Jones was an artist and poet. He studied at Camberwell School of Art in London and then joined the Royal Welsh Fusiliers during World War I. He studied again after the war and joined Eric Gill at his community of artists and craftsmen in Sussex. There he learnt to engrave and he began to illustrate books. He later painted in watercolours and also wrote poems. His most famous volume, *In Parenthesis*, was published in 1937.

Ken Kiff (1935–2001)
Clown
Made between 1996–9, measures 50.5 x 54.5 cm

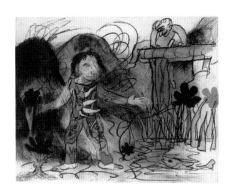

In this coloured etching a figure dressed in a clown-like costume decorated with faces and hands, stands pointing towards the water. A fish looks up at him.
In the background another person holding a mallet or hammer climbs carefully into the scene. The dark hills, scrawled clouds and huge reed-like flowers seem as alive as the characters.

    Ken Kiff drew, painted and made prints. He described the subject matter of his work as 'the music that can arise from working with the materials'. He was born in Essex and went to Hornsey School of Art in London. From 1992–4 he was Associate Artist at the National Gallery.

Pietro Longhi (1701–1785)
Exhibition of a Rhinoceros at Venice
Probably painted in 1751, measures 60.4 x 47 cm

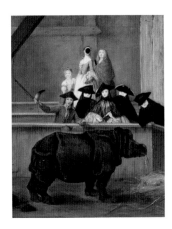

The rhinoceros was a new and strange creature in Europe when this picture was painted. The one shown here was brought to Venice in 1751 for the annual carnival and was exhibited for the public to see. While the keeper holds the animal's horn in the air the spectators, some in carnival masks, peer at the beast or gaze out at us, the viewers.

    Pietro Longhi worked in Venice. He painted small scenes of aristocratic and bourgeois life.

Adolphe Monticelli (1824–1886)
Torchlight Procession
Probably painted between 1870–86, measures 30.5 x 48.9 cm

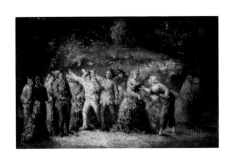

A celebration seems to be taking place; perhaps the richly costumed figures are taking part in a carnival while fireworks explode in the dark night sky above them. The procession has stopped for a moment to watch a conversation between the two figures on the right, but a man in white urges them onwards.

    Adolphe Monticelli was born in Marseilles but studied in Paris. He spent many hours in the Louvre, learning from the works of artists such as Rembrandt, Titian and the eighteenth-century painter Jean-Antoine Watteau. His characteristic swirling effects in thickly daubed paint were much admired by later artists such as Van Gogh.

François de Nomé (about 1593–after 1630)
Fantastic Ruins with Saint Augustine and the Child
Painted in 1623, measures 45.1 x 66 cm

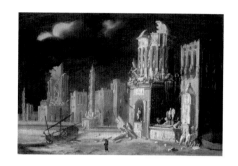

Night in an imaginary city of grand but crumbling buildings is the scene for this painting of the fourth-century Saint Augustine. Augustine walks along the seashore meditating on the Trinity (of God the Father, Son and Holy Spirit) when he meets a small child who is trying to empty the sea into a hole dug in the sand with a seashell. When Augustine remarks that this is an impossible task, the child – who represents the Christ Child – replies that Augustine is doing something even more impossible by trying to explain the Trinity.

François de Nomé came from Metz in eastern France, but worked in Rome and Naples in Italy. He painted mainly architectural and nocturnal scenes.

Emily Mary Osborn (1834–about 1893)
Nameless and Friendless
Painted in 1857, measures 82.5 x 104.2 cm

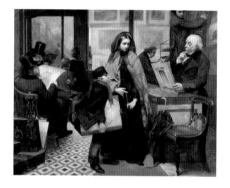

A young woman artist has walked with a child (perhaps her son or her young brother) through the rain to an art dealer and is trying to sell her work. She seems to be poor and unmarried, as she has no wedding ring.

We notice her unhappy expression first, but it is hard to tell what the dealer thinks of her work. Is he impressed, or doubtful of its quality? His assistant on the ladder has certainly stopped to look. The two men on the left, however, are more interested in the young woman than in her art.

This picture perhaps also hints at the difficulties women painters had in becoming professionals. But Emily Mary Osborn was actually painting at a time when women began to have greater access to art education and opportunities to exhibit their paintings. She showed work at the Royal Academy in London when she was still a teenager. By 1855 she had important portrait commissions and she sold a picture to Queen Victoria. She became best known for the somewhat sentimental appeal of her scenes from everyday life.

Piero di Cosimo (about 1462–after 1515)

A Satyr mourning over a Nymph

Painted in about 1495, measures 65.4 x 184.2 cm

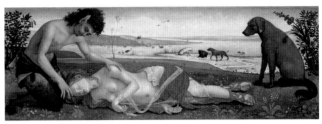

A seemingly lifeless nymph lies on the grass with wounded hand, wrist and throat. A kneeling satyr – half-goat, half-man – bends tenderly over her while a dog sits at her feet. In the background other creatures, including a pelican and more dogs, play about on the shore. We do not know the exact story this picture tells, but it could be connected with the tale of Procris and Cephalus from the Latin poet Ovid's *Metamorphoses*. Procris was accidentally killed by Cephalus, her husband, while he was out hunting.

Piero di Cosimo was the son of a Florentine goldsmith. His paintings often include panoramic landscapes rich in natural detail. The picture was probably originally a backboard for a bench or chest or part of the panelling of a Florentine palace.

The Quay Brothers (1947–)

Serenato in Vano

Made in 1970, measures 14.3 x 15.1 cm

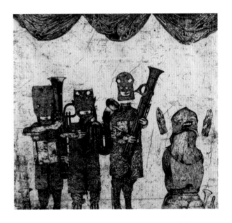

Three strange musicians are shown playing on unusual old instruments. They have face-like masks but no heads. On the right an armoured figure raises its hands, but it has no arms…

The Quay brothers are twins. They studied at Philadelphia College of Art in the United States and the Royal College of Art in London. Since 1980 they have worked on a wide range of projects including puppet-animation and live-action films, as well as set designs for opera, theatre and ballet productions. They have created films for television including collaborations with the composer Karlheinz Stockhausen and the choreographer Will Tuckett. The etching *Serenato in Vano* is an early work from their time at the Royal College of Art.

Paula Rego (1935–)
Sleeping
Painted in 1986, measures 150 x 150 cm

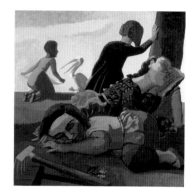

In a mysterious scene, two girls lie fast asleep on the ground while a third leans wearily against a tree. A fourth girl watches a pelican walk by against a pale, bright background. A rake and sprig of mistletoe seem to have been tossed down by the sleeping girls. Like many of Paula Rego's works this picture tells a particular story, but Rego encourages viewers to think up their own stories too.

According to the artist, this picture is about the Agony in the Garden, an episode in the life of Jesus described in the Bible (Mark 14:32–50; John 18:1–12). Before Jesus was arrested and eventually crucified, he took three of his disciples to the Mount of Olives to pray. He walked a little way from them where an angel appeared to him. When he returned to the disciples they had fallen asleep and he told them off. Here the disciples have become 'naughty girls', asleep when they should have been awake, a garden tool lying useless beside them. In Christian imagery the pelican symbolises the sacrifice Christ made on the cross.

Paula Rego was born in Portugal and spent her childhood there. She now lives in England.

Gabriel-Jacques de Saint-Aubin (1724–1780)
A Street Show in Paris
Painted in 1760, measures 80 x 64.1 cm

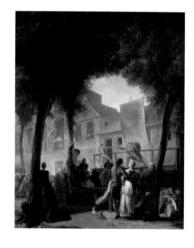

On this stage in a city street, two men fight a mock duel. The audience around them react to the event in different ways: a woman with a pink parasol peers at the scene from her balcony, but the man next door looks as if he would rather the play took place in front of someone else's house. Others seem more interested in their own private dramas than in the one taking place on the stage.

Gabriel-Jacques de Saint-Aubin lived and died in Paris. He made few paintings and is best known for his engravings and drawings.

Giovanni Domenico Tiepolo (1727–1804)
The Building of the Trojan Horse
Painted in about 1760, measures 38.8 x 66.7 cm

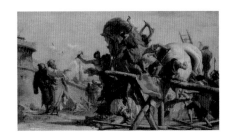

The ancient Greeks laid siege to the city of Troy for nearly ten years. In a final attempt to gain access to the city they built a wooden horse in which they hid their troops. Here men are building furiously, working on the wooden structure with hammers and chisels. The city walls are visible in the background, and the men on the left may be the Greek heroes Agamemnon and Odysseus. This picture was probably painted as a sketch in preparation for a larger painting of the same subject.

Giovanni Domenico Tiepolo was born in Venice, but he also worked in Würzburg in Germany and Madrid. His father and brother were also painters.

Paolo Uccello (1397–1475)
Saint George and the Dragon
Painted in about 1460, measures 56.5 x 74 cm

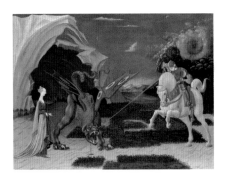

This picture shows two episodes from the legend of Saint George. He is said to have lived in the third century and was made patron saint of England in 1222.

Saint George defeated a dragon that had been terrorising the inhabitants of a city, rescuing a princess the dragon had captured. The princess then led the dragon through the city using her blue belt as a lead. This dragon is a strange-looking beast: Uccello has painted it without arms, and with odd markings on its wings. In the sky a whirlwind storm gathers, perhaps suggesting Saint George had divine assistance. There is also a tiny crescent moon gleaming above the saint's head. The 'doormat' patches of grass help to give a sense of perspective, something that always fascinated Uccello.

Paolo Uccello's real name was Paolo Doni, but he was called Uccello (which means bird in Italian) because he was supposed to have loved birds. He worked mainly in Florence painting pictures on wood panels, canvas and walls.

Gabrielle Vincent (1928–2000)
From Ernest est Malade
Published in 1987

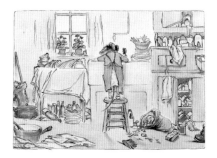

A mouse dressed in a child's clothes and an apron stands on a stool at an old-fashioned sink surrounded by kitchen disorder. The mouse is Célestine. She and a bear called Ernest appear in a series of twenty-five books by the Belgian illustrator Gabrielle Vincent. The stories in which they appear are based on the simple events of everyday life.

Gabrielle Vincent died in 2000 at the age of 72. She was also a painter under her own name, Monique Martin. Although she illustrated numerous books, she is best known as the creator of Ernest et Célestine.

Józef Wilkon (1930–)
From *Bats in the Belfry*
Published in 1985

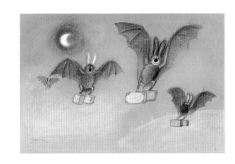

A family of smiling bats carry suitcases and parcels through an orange moonlit sky.

The illustration is taken from *Bats in the Belfry*, written by Eveline Hasler, in which a fire forces a family of bats to leave their bell-tower home. As nocturnal creatures, they are under pressure to find dark shelter before daybreak. This picture shows their delight as they discover a house with an open attic window.

Józef Wilkon is one of the most famous Polish illustrators of books for children. He employs a wide variety of techniques, showing in particular – as in this picture – a painterly and improvisational use of pastels. You can find illustrations by him in many books, including *Flowers for the Snowman* and *The Story of the Kind Wolf*.

Harmen Steenwyck (1612–after 1655)
X-ray of *Still life: An Allegory of the Vanities of Human Life*
Painted in about 1640, measures 39.2 x 50.7 cm

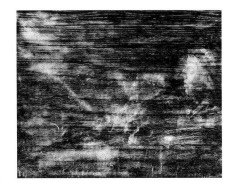

This image is an X-ray of a painting. X-rays can help scientists discover how a painting was made by penetrating layers of paint to reveal ideas or plans the artist might have subsequently painted over. In the X-ray of this picture by the Dutch artist Harmen Steenwyck you can see a ghostly face under the bottle on the right. Steenwyck started by painting a bust or portrait, probably of a Roman emperor, but he must have changed his mind about it and painted a bottle over the top. When the painting was new the face would have been invisible, but because oil paints become more transparent over time, today the face is visible even to the naked eye.

This collection of objects is meant to symbolise those aspects of human life and activities that were thought to be vain and futile in comparison with the lasting truths of religion. The books stand for human knowledge; the musical instruments – a recorder, a shawm (a kind of oboe) and lute – for the pleasures of the senses. The Japanese sword and shell, which would have been expensive rarities in the seventeenth century, stand for wealth, and the skull, the timepiece and the extinguished lamp for the transience and frailty of human life.

Jack B. Yeats (1871–1957)
The Double Jockey Act
Painted in 1916, measures 61 x 46 cm

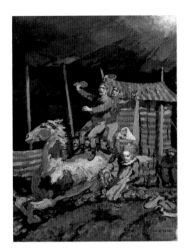

Two bareback riders balance on a piebald horse that is cantering round the ring of a travelling circus. A clown gallops crazily alongside the horse, imitating both the men and the animal. On the right, a countryman stares intensely at the scene. The picture is painted in thick oil paint with broad brushstrokes.

Jack Yeats was part of a great artistic Irish family which included his father, the portrait painter, John Butler Yeats, his brother the poet William Butler Yeats, and his sisters Lily, a painter and embroiderer, and Elizabeth, also a painter. He grew up in Sligo, Ireland, and started his career as a book illustrator. Later he painted in oils, specialising in landscapes and scenes of Irish life.

Lisbeth Zwerger (1954–)
From *Dwarf Nose*
Published in 1993

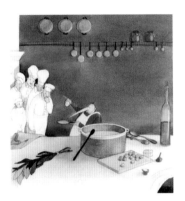

A squat man with an enormous nose stands behind a huge metal tureen surrounded by ingredients and utensils. This bizarre figure with a copper frying pan and a shaker is watched by five doubtful-looking chefs.

Lisbeth Zwerger was born in Vienna and has been a freelance illustrator since 1977 when her first book, *The Strange Child*, was published. She has continued to illustrate classic texts by authors such as the Brothers Grimm, Hans Christian Andersen, Charles Dickens and Lewis Carroll. Her illustrations are distinguished by her characteristic and elegant sense of draughtsmanship and design. *Dwarf Nose* is by Wilhelm Hauff.

Where to find the pictures

A Hendrick Avercamp, *A Winter Scene with Skaters near a Castle*, is from the National Gallery, London

B John Burningham's picture is from the book *Oi! Get off our Train*, published by Jonathan Cape, 1989 (© John Burningham. Photo: National Gallery, London)

C Emma Chichester Clark, *A Love Affair*, is from a private collection (© Emma Chichester Clark. Photo: National Gallery, London)

D Honoré-Victorin Daumier, *Don Quixote and Sancho Panza*, is from the National Gallery, London

E Adam Elsheimer, *Saint Paul on Malta*, is from the National Gallery, London

F Michael Foreman's picture is from the book *Seasons of Splendour*, published by Pavilion, 1985 (© Michael Foreman. Photo: National Gallery, London)

G Francisco de Goya, *A Scene from El Hechizado por Fuerza ('The Forcibly Bewitched')*, is from the National Gallery, London

H Edward Hopper, *Night in the Park*, is from The British Museum, London (© Photo: The British Museum, London)

I Roberto Innocenti's picture is from the book *The Adventures of Pinocchio*, published by Jonathan Cape, 1988 (© Roberto Innocenti. Photo: Roberto Innocenti, Florence)

J David Jones, *The Garden Enclosed*, is from the Tate, London (© Trustees of the David Jones Estate. Photo: Tate 2001)

K Ken Kiff, *Clown*, is from Marlborough Graphics, London (© successors of Ken Kiff. Photo: courtesy of Marlborough Graphics, London)

L Pietro Longhi, *Exhibition of a Rhinoceros at Venice*, is from the National Gallery, London

M Adolphe Monticelli, *Torchlight Procession*, is from the National Gallery, London

N François de Nomé, *Fantastic Ruins with Saint Augustine and the Child*, is from the National Gallery, London

O Emily Mary Osborn, *Nameless and Friendless*, is from a private collection (© Photo: courtesy of the owner)

P Piero di Cosimo, *A Satyr mourning over a Nymph*, is from the National Gallery, London

Q The Quay Brothers, *Serenato in Vano*, is from a private collection (© The Quay Brothers. Photo: National Gallery, London)

R Paula Rego, *Sleeping*, is from the Arts Council Collection, Hayward Gallery, London (© Paula Rego. Photo: courtesy of the Arts Council Collection, Hayward Gallery, London)

S Gabriel-Jacques de Saint-Aubin, *A Street Show in Paris*, is from the National Gallery, London

T Giovanni Domenico Tiepolo, *The Building of the Trojan Horse*, is from the National Gallery, London

U Paolo Uccello, *Saint George and the Dragon*, is from the National Gallery, London

V Gabrielle Vincent's picture is from the book *Ernest est Malade*, published by Duculot, 1987 (© Gabrielle Vincent. Courtesy of Casterman Editions, Brussels. Photo: National Gallery, London)

W Józef Wilkon's picture is from the book *Bats in the Belfry*, published by Bohem Press Kinderverlag, 1985 (© Józef Wilkon. Courtesy of Bohem Press, Zurich. Photo: National Gallery, London)

X Harmen Steenwyck, X-ray of *Still Life: An Allegory of the Vanities of Human Life*, is from the National Gallery, London

Y Jack B. Yeats, *The Double Jockey Act*, is from The National Gallery of Ireland, Dublin (© Successors of Jack B. Yeats. Photo: National Gallery of Ireland, Dublin)

Z Lisbeth Zwerger's picture is from the book *Dwarf Nose*, published by North-South Books (© Lisbeth Zwerger. Photo: courtesy of Nord-Süd Verlag, Zurich)

All pictures © National Gallery, London unless otherwise stated

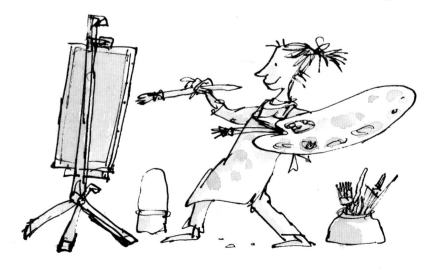

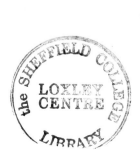